SHEPHERD'S NOTES

SHEPHERD'S NOTES

Bible Summary Series

Life & Teachings of Jesus

BROADMAN
&HOLMAN
PUBLISHERS

Nashville, Tennessee

Shepherd's Notes—*The Life and Teachings of Jesus*
© 2000
by Broadman & Holman Publishers
Nashville, Tennessee
All rights reserved
Printed in the United States of America

0–8054–9384–0
Dewey Decimal Classification: 232.9
Subject Heading: Jesus Christ—Biography.
Library of Congress Card Catalog Number: 99–054018

**Dedicated to Jimmy and Nancy Carter
who humbly try to live for Jesus**

Library of Congress Cataloging-in-Publication Data
Gould, Dana, 1951–.
    The life and teachings of Jesus / by Dana Gould and Terry Miethe.
        p. cm. — (Shepherd's notes.)
    Includes bibliographical references.
    ISBN 0–8054–9384–0
    1. Jesus Christ—Biography. 2. Jesus Christ—Teachings. I. Title. II. Series.
    BT301.2.G95 2000
    232.9'01—dc21   99–054018
                                                                                    CIP

1 2 3 4 5 6   03 02 01 00
R

CONTENTS

Dear Reader:

Shepherd's Notes are now available on every book in the Bible. In addition, we are pleased to provide a number of volumes in what we call **The Bible Summary Series**. This series will give you a perspective on various parts of the Bible that you wouldn't get by focusing on a book at time. These volumes include *Old Testament, New Testament, Life & Teachings of Jesus, Life & Letters of Paul, Basic Christian Beliefs,* and *Manners & Customs of Bible Times.*

This particular volume, *Life & Teachings of Jesus* by Dana Gould and Terry Miethe, provides a quick and easy-to-read overview of Jesus' life in chronological order, based on A. T. Robertson's *Harmony of the Gospels. Life & Teachings of Jesus* complements other volumes of *Shepherd's Notes* including a number of volumes on Christian classics. You can find a complete listing of all *Shepherd's Notes* on the back cover.

It's our prayer that *Shepherd's Notes* will serve you well as you read and live God's Word.

In Him,

David R. Shepherd
Editor-in-Chief

HOW TO USE THIS BOOK

DESIGNED FOR THE BUSY USER

Shepherd's Notes is designed to provide an easy-to-use tool for getting a quick handle on a Bible book's important features and, in the case of this volume, of gaining an understanding of the life and teachings of Jesus. Information available in more difficult-to-use reference works has been incorporated into the *Shepherd's Notes* format. This brings you the benefits of many more advanced and expensive works packed into one small volume.

Shepherd's Notes are for laymen, pastors, teachers, small-group leaders and participants, as well as the classroom student. Enrich your personal study or quiet time. Shorten your class or small-group preparation time as you gain valuable insights in the truths of God's Word that you can pass along to your students or group members.

DESIGNED FOR QUICK ACCESS

Those with time constraints will especially appreciate the timesaving features built in the *Shepherd's Notes*.

Concise Information. Shepherd's Notes—Life and Teachings of Jesus is replete with characters, places, events, and teachings that will enrich believers. Short sections provide quick "snapshots" of Jesus' life and mission.

Icons. Various icons in the margin highlight recurring themes in Jesus' teachings and aid in selective searching or tracing of those themes.

Sidebars and Charts. These specially selected features provide additional background information for your study or preparation. These include definitions as well as cultural, historical, and biblical insights.

In addition to the above features, for those readers who require or desire more information and resources for studying the life of Jesus, a list of reference sources used for this volume, suggests many works that will allow the reader to extend the scope of his or her study of Jesus and His teachings.

DESIGNED TO WORK FOR YOU

Personal Study. Using the *Shepherd's Notes* with a passage of Scripture can enlighten your study and take it to a new level. At your fingertips is information that would require searching several volumes to find. In addition, many points of application occur throughout the volume, contributing to personal growth.

Teaching. A running outline frames the text of the life of Jesus. Historical Context and others icons indicate where background information is supplied.

Group Study. Shepherd's Notes can be an excellent companion volume to use for gaining a quick but accurate understanding of Jesus and His teachings. The *Note's* format provides a summary of Jesus' life and influence that is helpful in doing a more detailed study in the Gospels.

LIST OF MARGIN ICONS USED IN THE LIFE AND TEACHINGS OF JESUS

Historical Context. To indicate background information—historical, biographical, cultural—and provide insight on the understanding or interpretation of a passage.

Old Testament Passage. To indicate a prophecy fulfillment and its discussion in the text.

New Testament Passage. To indicate a New Testament passage that illuminates Jesus' life and teachings.

Quote. To identify an enlightening quote pertinent to the discussion of the text.

Word Picture. To define or illustrate the meaning of a specific word or phrase to shed light on the passage in which it occurs.

This brief treatment of the life and ministry of Christ follows the order of events provided in A. T. Robertson's *A Harmony of the Gospels*, a standard in the study of the Gospels. The reader may choose to use Robertson's work in tandem with this brief description to gain a more in-depth study on special events and topics covered by this material.

JESUS' EARLY LIFE - - - -

The Preexistence of Christ
(John 1:1–18)

In one sense Jesus' life began when He was conceived by the Holy Spirit in the womb of His mother, Mary. But in a far larger sense, His life had no beginning. Jesus Christ, the Word who was with God and was God, has always existed. This truth is stated in the familiar words of John's Gospel.

In the beginning was the Word, and the Word was with God, and the Word was God. He was with God in the beginning. All things were created through Him, and apart from Him not one thing was created that has been created (John 1:1–3, HCSB).

The One who created every elementary particle and every galaxy became a human being. For thirty-three years He lived (*tabernacled*) among men. Literally, He "pitched His tent" among us. John says that in Him "we have seen his glory, the glory of the only Son of the Father" (v. 14, NLT)

Logos

Logos is a Greek word, rich in meaning, which appears forty times in John's Gospel. In this context it denotes God's revealing Himself.

Jesus' Family Tree
(Matt. 1:1–17; Luke 3:23–38)

Jesus became a man at a specific place and time and in a particular culture. As a man, Jesus had a family tree as all of us do. Matthew and Luke traced Jesus' human lineage in different ways.

One motive of tracing a lineage is to show purity of the bloodlines. In Jesus' genealogy are some notorious sinners and some persons who were not Hebrews. Perhaps Matthew included these to show Jesus' identification with sinners and His care for Gentiles, persons who seemed to be beyond the pale of God's redemption. What is your response to Jesus' identifying with sinful human beings?

Matthew traced Jesus' genealogy through his foster-father, Joseph, back to Abraham. Matthew emphasized that Jesus was both son of David and son of Abraham. Luke, on the other hand, is believed to have traced Jesus' lineage through Mary, His mother, back to Adam.

Two Birth Announcements
(Luke 1:5–80; Matt.1:18–25)

In 7 or 6 B.C., within a period of six months, the angel Gabriel made two appearances in Israel. Gabriel first appeared to a priest named Zechariah who was officiating during the time of morning prayer at the Temple in Jerusalem. Zechariah's reaction was fear. Gabriel told him not to be afraid. He told Zechariah that his and his wife Elizabeth's prayers of many years were going to be answered. They were going to have a son. He was to be named John.

Gabriel said that John would prepare God's people for the long-awaited Messiah. For Zechariah, this was too good to be true. Zechariah and Elizabeth were well past the childbearing years. He asked Gabriel how he could know that these events would take place. Gabriel told Zechariah that he would be unable to speak until John was born.

Within six months Gabriel appeared in Nazareth of Galilee to a virgin named Mary. She was engaged to a man named Joseph, a descendent of David. Like Zechariah, Mary was frightened by Gabriel's visit. Gabriel quickly sought to ease Mary's fears by telling her that she had found favor with God. She was to be the mother of God's Son and was to name Him Jesus.

Mary asked Gabriel how this could be since she had never known a man. Gabriel told her this would be a work of God's Spirit. Mary

Jesus

Jesus is the Greek form of *Joshua,* meaning "Jahweh is salvation."

responded by expressing her willingness to do whatever God was asking of her.

Soon after this, Mary went up to Judah to the home of her cousin Elizabeth, wife of Zechariah. Elizabeth was in her sixth month of pregnancy. When Mary spoke to Elizabeth, the child in Elizabeth's womb leaped for joy. Three months later, when Elizabeth gave birth, they asked his father what his name was to be. Zechariah wrote on a tablet that he was to be called John. At that moment, Zechariah's speech was restored.

Mary and Joseph. Gabriel had spoken to Mary, and she had responded in faith and obedience, but what about Joseph, the man to whom she was engaged? He learned that she was going to have a child. This raised many questions in Joseph's mind. He had a choice of two courses of action. He could bring the matter to light, which likely would have resulted in Mary's being stoned, or he could put her away privately.

Joseph chose the second alternative. But as he began to take this action, God spoke to Joseph in a dream and told him he should have no fear in proceeding with his marriage to Mary. The child in her womb had been conceived by the Holy Spirit. Joseph was to call the child Jesus.

Jesus' Birth (Luke 2:1–20)

As the time of Mary's delivery approached, Joseph and Mary journeyed from Nazareth to Joseph's ancestral home in Bethlehem. Caesar Augustus, emperor of Rome, had decreed a census that would be used in taxing both citizens and subjects of Rome. While they were in Bethlehem for this census, Mary gave birth to her Son in a stable. The village was so crowded that this was the only alternative.

Mary is Jesus' mother, and she is His disciple. Her willingness to be available to God for His purposes is a model for all other followers of Jesus. Daily is not too often to check our willingness to say, "I am the Lord's servant, and I am willing to accept whatever He wants. May everything you have said come true" (Luke 1:38, NLT).

This census was likely decreed in 8 B.C., but two years elapsed before it took effect in Judea.

On the night of Jesus' birth, angels appeared to shepherds in the vicinity of Bethlehem. They announced the birth of a Savior, the long-awaited Messiah. Following this dramatic visitation, the shepherds ran to Bethlehem to see the child for themselves.

Jesus—Born Under the Law (Luke 2:21–38)

Justin Martyr observed that Jesus' circumcision is an example of His full obedience to the law.

When Jesus was eight days old, Joseph and Mary took Him on the five-mile journey up to Jerusalem to be circumcised according to the Law of Moses. On this occasion He was formally given the name Jesus.

Forty days after His birth, Jesus' parents returned to the Temple to dedicate Jesus and complete the purification required of women following the birth of a child. Jesus and His parents were greeted by two aged saints, Simeon and Anna, who had looked for the One God had promised Israel.

Joseph's offering of two doves and two pigeons as a sacrifice indicates that he couldn't afford to offer a lamb.

Simeon thanked God that he was able to live to see God's salvation and said that he could now die in peace. Simeon blessed Jesus and spoke prophetically to Mary when he said that a sword would pierce her heart because of the reaction to her Son. When the aged prophetess Anna saw the young child, she thanked God and spread the word about Him to those who were like-minded in the Temple.

The Magi Visit Jesus (Matt. 2:1–23; Luke 2:39)

For a time Joseph and Mary apparently chose to return to Bethlehem rather than go back to Nazareth. While they were living there, Magi from the East came to Jerusalem looking for the young child. They had seen His star and followed it in order to pay homage to Him. The Magi inquired of Herod about the young child, and Herod, in turn, asked the chief priests and scribes.

They told Herod that the Messiah was to be born in Bethlehem. Herod charged the Magi to come back and tell him when they found the young king so that he could come and worship Him. The star that led the Magi to Jerusalem guided them from Jerusalem to Bethlehem to the house where Jesus lived. They entered the house and worshiped Him, presenting gifts of gold, frankincense, and myrrh.

But as for you, Bethlehem Ephrathah, too little to be among the clans of Judah, from you One will go forth for Me to be ruler in Israel. His goings forth are from long ago, from the days of eternity (Mic. 5:2, NASB).

God warned the Magi through a dream not to return to their home by way of Jerusalem. God also warned Joseph in a dream to take Mary and Jesus and flee to Egypt to avoid the wrath of Herod.

When Herod realized the Magi had not complied with his request, he had all of the male children in Bethlehem two years and under put to death. The Scriptures give no indication of how long Joseph kept his family in Egypt, but he did so until God gave him directions to return to Nazareth.

Jesus' Childhood (Luke 2:40–52)

The Gospels give us little information about Jesus as a boy. Luke tells of a time when Jesus was twelve years old. His parents took Him to Jerusalem to celebrate Passover. As they began their return trip to Nazareth, they became aware that He wasn't among them. So they returned to Jerusalem and found Him in the Temple listening to the teachers and asking them questions. Mary asked Jesus why He had caused them to worry by staying behind in Jerusalem. Jesus responded with surprise. He thought they knew that He needed to be about His Father's business. Knowing how special He was, they still didn't understand this.

Then he returned to Nazareth with them and was obedient to them; and his mother stored all these things in her heart. So Jesus grew in both height and wisdom, and he was loved by God and by all who knew him (Luke 2:51–52, NLT).

JOHN THE BAPTIST'S MINISTRY

The Time (Mark 1:1; Luke 3:1–2)

Luke says that the Word of God came to John in the fifteenth year of the reign of Tiberius Caesar or in A.D. 26. John lived in the wilderness of Judea. He dressed in camel's hair and ate a simple diet of locusts and wild honey.

John's Message (Mark 1:2–8; Matt. 3:1–12; Luke 3:3–18)

John baptized in the Jordan and preached repentance to the people of Jerusalem and Judea who came to hear him. John was especially tough on the religious leaders whom he called snakes. They believed their lineage gave them right standing with God. He warned them of coming judgment and urged them to change their outlook and way of living. John saw himself as preparing the way for Israel's Messiah. He strongly emphasized that he was not the Messiah and was unworthy to untie the Messiah's shoes.

John uses a picture from farming to convey what was about to happen. "His [Messiah's] winnowing fork is in His hand to thoroughly clear His threshing floor, and to gather the wheat into His barn; but He will burn up the chaff with unquenchable fire" (Luke 3:17, NASB).

Jesus Begins His Public Ministry

John Baptizes Jesus (Late Summer, A.D. 26) (Mark 1:9–11; Matt. 3:13–17; Luke 3:21–23)

Jesus journeyed from His home village of Nazareth to Judea where John was preaching and baptizing. John recognized Jesus as one who did not need to repent and be baptized. Rather, John said he needed to be baptized by Jesus. But Jesus insisted that John should baptize Him in order to fulfill all righteousness.

As Jesus was baptized, the heavens opened, and the Holy Spirit descended on Jesus in the form of a dove. A voice spoke from heaven, "You are my Son, whom I love; with you I am well pleased" (Luke 3:22)

Jesus Is Tempted (Mark 1:12–13; Matt. 4:1–11; Luke 4:1–13)

Immediately following His baptism, the Spirit led Jesus into the wilderness to be tempted by Satan. Jesus fasted over a period of forty days. As a result, He was hungry. Satan told Him if He were the Son of God, He could command the stones around Him to become bread. To counter this temptation, Jesus quoted God's Word: "Man does not live by bread alone, but man lives by everything that proceeds out of the mouth of the LORD" (Deut. 8:3, NASB).

In the second temptation, Satan took Jesus to the pinnacle of the Temple in Jerusalem and urged Him to make a spectacular jump. Satan even quoted Scripture to the effect that God would send His angels to keep Jesus from being hurt. Jesus, recognizing that Satan was misapplying Scripture, came back—once again

"The dove is symbolic of gentleness, innocence and meekness. Furthermore, the Levitical law prescribed one dove, along with a lamb, or two doves only for the poor, as a sacrificial offering. So the anointing of Jesus by the Spirit in the form of a dove foretold His ministry as a sacrifice for sin, and the Father's approval of the Son further attested His sinless purity as a fit offering for sin"—Hobbs, *The Life and Times of Jesus,* 36.

Satan

Satan is a Hebrew word whose Greek equivalent is *diablos* translated "devil." Both terms picture him as an accuser.

Each of the Scriptures Jesus quoted to Satan were from Deuteronomy, where Israel, in its journey from Egypt through the wilderness to Canaan had succumbed to numerous temptations. Jesus resisted Satan's three temptations by relying on God's written Word. Today Christians are strengthened to resist temptation as they know and live by God's Word.

quoting from Deuteronomy: "You shall not put the LORD your God to the test, as you tested Him at Massah" (Deut. 6:16, NASB).

In the third temptation Satan offered Jesus the kingdoms of the Earth if Jesus would bow and worship Satan. For the third time Jesus relied on Scripture: "Get out of here, Satan . . . for the Scriptures say, 'You must worship the Lord your God; serve only him'" (Matt. 4:10, NLT).

John the Baptist and Jesus (John 1:19–34)

While John was preaching in the wilderness of Judea, a committee of priests and Levites from Jerusalem were sent to him to inquire as to whether he might be the Messiah. John strongly denied that he was the Messiah. He did indicate that among them was one to whom John was not worthy to be a servant.

The next day John saw Jesus and described Him as "the Lamb of God, who takes away the sin of the world." God had enabled John to recognize Jesus as the Messiah at Jesus' baptism, with the descent of the Holy Spirit in the form of a dove.

Jesus Begins to Call Disciples (John 1:35–51)

Later that day, John was with two of his disciples. Seeing Jesus, John said to his disciples that Jesus is the Lamb of God. John's disciples left him immediately to follow Jesus. As Jesus was preparing to leave Judea and return to Galilee, He called two other disciples, Philip and Nathanael.

Jesus' First Miracle (John 2:1–12)

Having returned to Galilee, Jesus, His mother, and His disciples attended a wedding in the village of Cana, only a few miles from Nazareth. Here Jesus performed His first miracle.

Jesus' First Cleansing of the Temple
(John 2:13–22)

A. T. Robertson called the period between Jesus' baptism and Passover of A.D 27, "The Year of Obscurity." Only John's Gospel records these events. Jesus came to Jerusalem in the spring of A.D 27 for the Feast of Passover. Jesus was greatly offended by the practices He saw in the Temple. A place of prayer and worship had become a marketplace. Jesus made a whip and drove both men and animals from the Temple. He overturned the tables of the moneychangers.

Conversation with Nicodemus
(John 2:23–3:21)

Many people, seeing the miracles Jesus performed in Jerusalem, believed in Him, but Jesus did not give Himself to them, knowing what was in their hearts. He did, however, receive one of the key religious leaders, a Pharisee named Nicodemus.

Nicodemus came to Jesus at night. He began by saying that he knew that Jesus was from God because of the miracles He was performing. Rather than engage in preliminary conversation, Jesus got right to the point. He told Nicodemus that in order to see the kingdom of God he had to be born again.

Nicodemus was thinking in terms of physical realities and asked Jesus how it was possible that a grown man could be born again. Jesus went on to say that He was talking about a spiritual birth.

Jesus gave Nicodemus a vivid illustration from Israel's history to help him understand how the new birth would take place. He said that just as Moses lifted up the snake on a pole, in the same way the Son of Man would be lifted up.

Most Jews in traveling between Judea and Galilee didn't take the most direct route—through Samaria. They crossed to the East side of the Jordan and went through Perea and then crossed to the West bank of the Jordan into Galilee. They wanted to avoid contact with Samaritans—a people who had intermarried with other people following the Assyrian conquest of Israel.

The forgiveness the Samaritan woman experienced turned her quickly from one who sought to be away from other people to a person who could not wait to be with others and tell them what Jesus had done for her. Jesus told her exactly who she was, but He spoke to save, not to condemn. How does Jesus' forgiveness of you affect your relationship with those around you?

Whoever believed on him would not die but have eternal life.

Ministry in Judea
(John 3:22–4:4; Luke 3:19–20; 4:14; Mark 1:14; Matt. 4:12)

Jesus spent a short time with His disciples ministering in a place not far from where John the Baptist was preaching and baptizing. Word of Jesus' successes came to the attention of the Pharisees in Jerusalem and raised their hostility toward Him. Also Jesus learned that Herod Antipas had arrested and imprisoned John the Baptist for John's criticism of his relationship with his brother's wife. So Jesus decided to leave Judea and return to Galilee.

Galilee Via Samaria
(John 4:5–45; Mark 1:14–15; Matt. 4:17; Luke 4:14–15)

Jesus took the route through Samaria on the way to Galilee. He stopped outside a village called Sychar about twenty-five miles north of Jerusalem. While His disciples went into Sychar to buy food, Jesus sat by Jacob's well. A Samaritan woman came to draw water. When Jesus asked her for a drink, a conversation began. The Samaritan woman wanted to talk in generalities. Jesus pressed the conversation to the specifics of her need. The result was that she came to accept Jesus as the Messiah.

At the Samaritans' request, Jesus stayed two days before traveling on to Galilee.

The people of Galilee had seen Jesus' miracles at the Passover in Jerusalem and so welcomed him as He came into their region.

THE GREAT GALILEAN MINISTRY

Healing an Official's Son
(John 4:46–54)

Jesus returned to the village of Cana where He had turned water into wine at a wedding feast. There the son of a royal official lay ill. When the man heard that Jesus had come to Cana, he sought Jesus out and urged Him to come and heal his son The official urged Jesus to come to his son before he died. Jesus assured the man that the boy would live.

"Unless you people see signs and wonders, you will not believe" (John 4:48, HCSB).

Rejection at Nazareth
(Luke 4:16–30)

Jesus returned to Nazareth, His home village. On the Sabbath He went to the synagogue and was invited to read from the book of Isaiah and comment on the passage. The initial reaction was favorable. The people of Nazareth took pride in this One who had grown up among them. As Jesus continued to speak, favor turned to fury. He cited two cases from the history of Israel where God showed mercy to Gentiles. This angered the congregation to the point where they threw Him out of Nazareth and took Him to a ledge and were going to throw Him down the hill. Luke says that Jesus simply walked through the crowd and escaped them.

The Spirit of the Sovereign LORD is upon me, because the LORD has appointed me to bring good news to the poor. He has sent me to comfort the brokenhearted and to announce that captives will be released and prisoners will be freed. He has sent me to tell those who mourn that the time of the LORD's favor has come, and with it, the day of God's anger against their enemies (Isa. 61:1–2, NLT).

On to Capernaum (Matt. 4:13–16, 18–22; Mark 1:16–20; Luke 5:1–11)

From Nazareth Jesus moved to Capernaum, the place where Simon Peter and others had settled and established their fishing business. At Capernaum, down on the shores of the Sea of Galilee, Jesus issued the call to two sets of brothers to leave their business and come be His disciples on a full-time basis. They had been His disciples during His days of ministry in Judea a year before. Now Jesus called Peter, Andrew, James, and John to leave all and follow Him.

Sabbath in Capernaum
(Mark 1:21–39; Luke 4:31–44;
Matt. 8:14–17, 23–25)

Jesus got a better reception at the synagogue in Capernaum than at Nazareth. The people were amazed at the authority with which He taught. As He was teaching, a demon-possessed man cried out. The demon recognized Jesus as the Holy One of God. Jesus commanded the demon to come out of the man. The demon threw the man to the ground and came out. The people who witnessed this event were all the more amazed at the authority of Jesus' word.

From the synagogue, Jesus and His disciples went to Simon Peter's house where his mother-in-law lay ill with a fever. Jesus touched her hand, and the fever left. She then ministered to the guests.

Word spread throughout Capernaum concerning Jesus and what He had done there. The result was that people brought those sick of body and mind to Peter's house, and Jesus healed them.

From Capernaum, Jesus and His first four disciples traveled throughout Galilee preaching the gospel of the kingdom and healing people with many kinds of diseases. Crowds not only from Galilee but also from Judea, Decapolis, and Perea began to follow Jesus.

Jesus Heals a Leper (Mark 1:40–45;
Matt. 8:2–4; Luke 5:12–16)

In the course of this ministry throughout Galilee, a leper approached Jesus. He expressed the confidence that Jesus had the power to heal him. His only question was whether Jesus would choose to heal him. Jesus told the leper that He wanted to heal him. When Jesus reached out, touched the man, and spoke the word, the leprosy left him.

Jesus charged the leper not to tell what had happened but to go to the priest and do all that was commanded in the Law. The man was so full of joy he could not help telling what had happened to him.

The Paralytic (Mark 2:1–12; Matt. 9:1–8; Luke 5:17–26)

Once, while Jesus was back in Capernaum, He was teaching in a home. His reputation had grown to the point that people flocked to the house to see Him and hear His teaching. Four men brought a friend who was paralyzed to the house on a pallet. The crowd was so large the friends were unable to enter the house by the door. So they climbed up on the roof, cut a hole in it, and lowered their friend into the presence of Jesus.

Jesus looked at the man and told him to be of good cheer—that his sins were forgiven. Jesus sensed that the religious leaders in the crowd were offended by His forgiving the paralyzed man's sins. Jesus asked them if it was easier to say, "Your sins are forgiven," or to say, "Rise, take up your bed, and walk."

Jesus said that to demonstrate that the Son of Man has power on earth to forgive sins, so He commanded the paralyzed man to take up his bed and walk. The man did just that. Those who witnessed this were amazed and gave glory to God.

For the Hebrews, leprosy was a dreaded disease that rendered its victims ceremonially unclean—unfit to worship God. Lepers were isolated from the community. Leprosy is sometimes a symbol for sin. Just as Jesus didn't hesitate to reach out and touch this leper, so He is able and willing to touch and cleanse us from sin. Jesus' power to heal lepers is one indication that He is the expected Messiah.

Capernaum was located strategically on the international highway that ran from Egypt to Damascus. Tax collection was an important business here since a duty had to be paid on all of the goods that passed over this highway. Tax collectors were among the most despised people in Jewish society. They profited from taking money from their fellow countrymen and putting it in the coffers of Rome.

Jesus Calls Matthew (Mark 2:13–17; Matt. 9:9–13; Luke 5:27–32)

Still in Capernaum, Jesus passed by the customs house and saw Matthew (Levi), a tax collector. Jesus commanded Matthew to follow Him. Matthew arose and followed Jesus. He hosted a party and invited his fellow tax collectors and friends to meet Jesus.

The religious leaders who saw this were highly critical of Jesus' associating with tax collectors.

Jesus Responds to Criticism (Mark 2:18–22; Matt. 9:14–17; Luke 5:33–39)

The list against Jesus was beginning to grow. He had, so they thought, committed blasphemy by forgiving sins. He was associating with unclean people. His disciples failed to fast. When asked about His disciples not fasting, Jesus responded by saying that while the bridegroom was present with the disciples they would feast. There would be a time for fasting when the bridegroom would be taken away. Jesus went on to say that He had not come to patch up an old garment or to put new wine into old wineskins. His hearers knew well from their own experience that these were not sound practices.

Controversy in Jerusalem (John 5:1–47)

Jesus and His disciples went to Jerusalem to attend a feast. It may well have been Passover in the spring of A.D. 28. On the Sabbath Jesus approached a pool called Bethesda that is located by the Sheep Gate. There He saw a man who had been crippled for thirty-eight years. Jesus asked the man if he wanted to be well. The man said he did but he had no one to take him to the pool when the water was stirred. Jesus then commanded the man to take up his bed and walk. He did.

You search the Scriptures because you believe they give you eternal life. But the Scriptures point to me! Yet you refuse to come to me so that I can give you this eternal life (John 5:39–40, NLT).

The Jewish leaders saw the man carrying his bed around on the Sabbath and asked him why he was violating the Law. The man said that he had just been healed and identified Jesus as the One who healed him. The religious leaders began to harass Jesus for what He had done.

Two Controversies Regarding the Sabbath (Mark 2:23–3:12; Matt. 12:1–21; Luke 6:1–11)

As Jesus and His disciples walked through grain fields on the Sabbath, the disciples picked heads of wheat and ate the grain. Some religious leaders saw this and criticized Jesus for allowing His disciples to violate the Sabbath Law. Jesus cited a case from the Scriptures where David and his men ate the bread that only the priests were supposed to eat.

It's probable that this event took place as Jesus and His disciples returned to Galilee from Jerusalem in the spring of A.D. 28 —A. T. Robertson, *A Harmony of the Gospels.*

Soon after this, Jesus was in a synagogue in Galilee on the Sabbath. There He encountered a man with a withered hand. Pharisees were watching carefully to see what Jesus would do. Jesus asked them whether it was lawful to do good on the Sabbath. They would not answer. Jesus then commanded the man with the withered hand to stretch it out; and as he did, the hand was restored. This ignited the fury of the Pharisees. From this point they worked with the Herodians to see how they could destroy Jesus.

Jesus sensed what was happening and withdrew with His disciples for a time. But this had the effect of causing the crowds to seek Him out even more. He healed the sick that were brought to Him.

Jesus Calls the Twelve (Mark 3:13–19; Luke 6:12–16)

With opposition against Jesus increasing, this was a critical time in His ministry. He spent all night in prayer and then called the twelve apostles to be those whom He would train, and to whom He would give the mission of doing what Jesus had begun.

The Sermon on the Mount
(Matt. 5:1–7:13; 8:1; Luke 6:17–49)

The Twelve, joined by others, began an intensive training process with instruction that has come to be called the Sermon on the Mount.

The first part of the sermon gives eight short descriptions of the kingdom of God.

Each of these eight descriptions affirms the happiness or blessedness of those who are part of the kingdom.

Next, Jesus compared kingdom standards with the Law given to Moses. Kingdom standards don't contradict the Law but reveal its true intent. Killing and adultery begin in the thought life before they are acted out. Jesus called His disciples to monitor carefully the contents of their heart.

Jesus contrasted the right use of prayer, fasting, and almsgiving with the hypocritical uses of these acts and called His disciples to a higher standard than those of the religious leaders of the day.

Jesus closed the Sermon on the Mount by setting forth two ways of living. One way leads to destruction, the other to eternal life. Everyone is walking one of these two paths.

Jesus Heals a Centurion's Servant, and a
Widow's Son Is Raised from the Dead
(Matt. 8:5–13; Luke 7:1–17)

Coming into Capernaum, a centurion who had a sick servant came to Jesus to ask Him to heal the servant. Jesus said He would go with the

Herschel Hobbs said the likely location for the Sermon on the Mount was the Horns of Hattin, a double-topped mountain between Capernaum and Nazareth.

"Looking back over these 'beatitudes' one sees a progression: conviction for sin; repentance for sin; committal to Christ; progressive development in righteousness; mercy toward others; sincerity of heart in constant fellowship with God; evangels of the Gospel to preach between God and man and between man and man; and patient endurance and joy as one experiences the enmity of the world"—Hobbs, *The Life and Times of Jesus*, 60.

centurion to the servant. But the centurion didn't think he was worthy to have Jesus in his house. He had great faith. Jesus told the centurion to go, and that because of his faith, his servant was healed.

When Jesus entered a city named Nain, the dead son of a widow was carried out to Him. This was the women's only son. Jesus told the dead son to "arise," and he sat up and began to talk. Jesus returned the son to his mother. Those present were gripped with fear and glorified God. They knew that God had sent a great prophet, and what happened at Nain soon spread throughout the whole of Judea.

Jesus' Fame Spreads Far and Wide
(Matt. 11:2–30; Luke 7:18–35)

So spread Jesus' fame that it reached John the Baptist in prison. John sent two disciples to ask Jesus if he was the One. That very hour, Jesus had cured many. Jesus told the men to go back to John and tell him what they had seen and heard: sight was restored to the blind, the lame were able to walk, lepers were cleansed, the deaf could hear, the dead were raised, and the poor had good news preached to them.

Jesus spoke to the large crowd about John, for he was the prophet who was to prepare the way for Jesus. But as great as John was, the one who is least in the kingdom of heaven is greater than John. Jesus said that John is Elijah who was to come (Mal. 4:5) and told His audience, "He who has ears to hear, let him hear" (Matt. 11:15, NASB).

Jesus Dines with a Pharisee (Luke 7:36–8:3)

While eating with Simon, a sinful woman brought a small alabaster jar of perfume; and as she cried, she wet Jesus' feet with her tears and wiped them with her hair, kissed His feet, and anointed them with the perfume.

Centurion

Centurion was the title of an officer in the Roman army who commanded one hundred men.

Alabaster

Alabaster (Matt. 26:7; Mark 14:3; Luke 7:37) frequently had a banded aspect of slightly varying shades and colors, often delicate and beautiful. This led to its frequently being called onyx among the ancients, and onyx marble and Mexican onyx today (though it is different, from true onyx). It was a favorite material for the little flasks and vases for ointment and perfume that are so abundant in Egyptian tombs because alabaster helped preserve the scent of the perfume.

Seeing the sinful woman do this, Simon said to himself, if Jesus really was a prophet, He would know what kind of woman was touching Him.

Jesus knew what Simon was thinking and told him the parable of the two debtors (Luke 7:40–43). Who would love the lender who forgave the two debts more? Answer: the one forgiven the larger debt.

Now Jesus turned to the woman and told the Pharisee that she had done many acts of kindness to Him that Simon did not. "For this reason I say to you, her sins, which are many, have been forgiven, for she loved much; but he who is forgiven little, loves little" (Luke 7:47, NASB). The others reclining at the table with Simon and Jesus wanted to know who this Man was who even forgave sins. Jesus told the woman to "go in peace" (v. 50) because her faith had saved her.

After the evening at Simon's house, Jesus made another (the second) tour of Galilee, this time with all twelve apostles. He was also accompanied by certain women, including Mary Magdalene, Joanna (wife of Cuza), and Susanna, and others who contributed to the group's support out of their private means.

Beelzebub

The name *Beelzebub* was used by the New Testament Jews to refer to the prince of demons (Matt. 12:24; cf. Matt. 9:34; Luke 11:15), and they accused Jesus of casting out demons by the power of Beelzebub.

A Chilling Accusation (Mark 3:19–30; Matt. 12:22–37)

Jesus' work stirred up great hatred among the Pharisees. They said that Jesus was in league with Satan. But Jesus asked them how Satan could cast out Satan? If a kingdom or a house is divided against itself, neither can stand.

Jesus warned against the sin that cannot be forgiven. Every sin and blasphemy can be forgiven except blasphemy against the Holy Spirit.

Demand for a Sign (Matt. 12:38–45)

The scribes and Pharisees asked for a sign. Jesus told them that the only sign for an "evil and adulterous generation" would be the sign of the prophet Jonah. So the Son of Man would be "three days and three nights in the heart of the earth" (Matt. 12:39–40).

Even Jesus' blood relatives feared that He was "beside Himself" from what they heard. Jesus said that whoever did the will of God was His brother, sister, and mother.

THE FIRST GREAT GROUP OF PARABLES

As Jesus sat by the seaside, a great crowd gathered around Him. So He got into a boat and spoke to them on the beach in parables. He taught them (1) the parable of the sower (Mark 4:3–25; Matt. 13:3–23; Luke 8:5–18); (2) the parable of the seed growing of itself (Mark 4:26–29); (3) the parable of the tares (Matt. 13:24–30); (4) the parable of the mustard seed (Mark 4:30–32, Matt. 13:31–32); (5) the parable of the leaven (Matt. 13:33–35), as well as a few others.

Later Jesus left the crowd and went into a house to talk to the disciples. There He gave the disciples an explanation of (1) the parable of the tares (Matt. 13:36–43); (2) the parable of the hidden treasure (Matt. 13:44); (3) the parable of the pearl of great price (Matt. 13:45–46); (4) the parable of the net (Matt. 13:47–50); and the parable of the householder (Matt. 13:51–53).

Jesus Calms a Storm (Mark 4:35–41; Matt. 8:18, 23–27; Luke 8:22–25)

On that same day, in the evening, Jesus and the disciples decided to cross to the other side of the sea. Jesus fell asleep as a great storm came up. When the boat began to fill with water, the

Parable

A *parable* is a short story embodying a message or moral by means of comparison. Jesus illustrated essential truths about the human condition in more than two dozen parables (some scholars count as many as sixty parables).

disciples were afraid they would die. They awakened Jesus for help. Jesus told the wind and the sea to be still, and there was a great calm. Then He asked the disciples why they had been afraid. The disciples marveled, and they asked one another who this was who could calm the wind and the sea.

Jesus Heals Demon-Possessed Men (Mark 5:1–20; Matt. 8:28–34; Luke 8:26–39)

Reaching the other side, they came to the country of the Gerasenes. A violent man who was demon-possessed met Him (Matthew relates two such men in 8:28). The man ran and worshiped Jesus and called Him "Son of the Most High God." Jesus commanded the demons named Legion—for many demons had entered him—to come out. The demons asked Jesus to allow them to enter a great herd of pigs feeding nearby. Immediately the whole herd, numbering about two thousand, rushed down into the sea and drowned.

Matthew mentions two demon-possessed men in 8:28 and conjectures that the one mentioned in Mark and Luke 'was probably the prominent and leading one'—A. T. Robertson, *A Harmony of the Gospels*.

Jesus Heals a Daughter and Encounters a Woman of Great Faith (Mark 5:21–43; Matt. 9:18–26; Luke 8:40–56)

Returning to the other side of the sea (probably in Capernaum), Jairus, one of the rulers of the synagogue, approached Jesus saying that his daughter was at the point of death.

On the way to Jairus' house, a woman who had a hemorrhage for twelve years came and touched the fringe of Jesus' outer garment and was immediately healed. Jesus felt the power leave Him and asked who had touched Him. The disciples thought it strange that Jesus, who was being pressed on all sides by the crowd, would ask who touched Him. When the woman revealed who she was, Jesus said to her:

"Daughter, your faith has made you well; go in peace, and be healed of your affliction" (Mark 5:34, NASB).

When Jesus and Peter and brothers James and John came to Jairus' house, the daughter was already dead. Jesus said that she was only sleeping, and those at the house laughed at Him. Entering the house, He took the child by the hand and said to her, *"Talitha koum!,"* which means, "Little girl, I say to you, get up!" (Mark 5:41). Immediately the twelve-year-old girl got up and walked. There was great amazement at this occurrence. Jesus told them not to tell others about this and to give the girl something to eat.

More Healings, Accusations, and a Last Visit to Nazareth (Matt. 9:27–34, 13:54–58; Mark 6:1–6)

Two blind men asked Jesus to have mercy on them. Jesus asked them if they believed He could heal them. They answered, "Yes." Jesus touched their eyes; and, because they believed, they could see again. Jesus told them not to say anything about the miracle, but they could not help but tell what had happened to them.

As the newly sighted men left, a dumb man possessed with a devil was brought to Jesus who cast out the devil. The people marveled because nothing like this had ever been seen in Israel. The Pharisees, of course, accused Jesus of casting out devils by the prince of the devils.

Jesus said to them, "A prophet is not without honor except in his hometown and in his household" (Matt. 13:57, HCSB).

Jesus went back to His hometown of Nazareth and began teaching them in the synagogue. The people were astonished and wondered where He got such wisdom and miraculous powers because they knew Him as a carpenter, the son of Mary, brother of James, Joseph,

Judas, and Simon, and His sisters, who still lived among them.

The people took offense because a prophet has no honor in his hometown. Jesus didn't do many miracles in Nazareth because of their unbelief.

The Third Tour of Galilee and the Twelve are Sent Forth Two by Two (Mark 6:6–13; Matt. 9:35–11:1; Luke 9:1–6)

Again Jesus went to the synagogues and taught and preached the gospel of the kingdom and healed every kind of disease and sickness. He saw that the people were distressed and downcast like sheep without a shepherd, and Jesus felt compassion for them.

Who will go out and come in before them, and who will lead them out and bring them in, that the congregation of the LORD may not be like sheep which have no shepherd (Num. 27:17, NASB; cf. Ezek. 34:5).

Jesus saw a large harvest but not many workers to gather the harvest. He asked His disciples to ask the Lord of the harvest to send out workers. Jesus then called the disciples together and gave them authority to cast out unclean spirits and to heal every kind of disease and sickness. He sent them forth two by two and charged them not to go to any Gentiles or any city of the Samaritans but only to the lost sheep of Israel. He gave them instructions for service (Matt. 10:1–15).

He further told them that a hard road was before them. They would be like sheep in the midst of wolves; therefore, they *must* [emphasis added] "be shrewd [*sharp, sly, quick, astute, intelligent*] as serpents and innocent as doves" (Matt.10:16, NASB).

"Everyone therefore who shall confess Me before men, I will also confess him before My Father who is in heaven (Matt. 10:32, NASB).

Jesus promised the apostles that they didn't need to worry when they were delivered to governors and kings, for the Spirit of the Father would give them what to say when they needed it. He told them that they would be hated by all on account of His name; but if they endured to the end, they would be saved.

A true disciple must be *like* his master but cannot be *above* him. Jesus warned His disciples that because they belonged to Him they would be rejected as He was. He urged them not to fear those who can kill the body; rather they should fear him who is able to destroy both soul and body in hell. Jesus reminded them that their Father knows when even a sparrow falls to the ground. He has even numbered the hairs of their heads.

Jesus reminded His disciples that His presence didn't bring peace on the earth but a sword. Being His disciple means putting Him ahead of all earthly relationships, including family. It requires taking up one's cross and dying to self in order to find life.

Herod Fears Jesus (Mark 6:14–29; Matt. 14:1–12; Luke 9:7–9)

Herod knew that John the Baptist was a righteous and holy man, and he feared him. But he had John beheaded because Herodias, his wife, hated John for denouncing her adulterous marriage to Herod. When Herod heard about Jesus, he feared that Jesus was John the Baptist raised from death.

The Apostles Return to Jesus and Five Thousand are Fed (Mark 6:30–44; Matt.14:13–21; Luke 9:10–17; John 6:1–13)

The Twelve came to Jesus and told Him all that they had done and taught. Jesus took them by boat to a desert place for rest because there were so many people coming and going that the disciples didn't even have time to eat.

The choice a believer has to make is not between God and Satan. The choice is between God and self. Satan's task is to influence us to choose self. Augustine saw this clearly in his day and wrote about it in his classic *The City of God.* It is by the character of our wills, and the character of our dominant love that we are ultimately marked. How are you marked? In which camp are you found? C. S. Lewis in *Mere Christianity* was correct. The very instant we have a "self," the possibility of putting that self at the center, of it wanting to be God, becomes a real possibility. Our choice is clear! To be truly free, to be truly ourselves, we must choose God over self.

But many people saw Jesus and the disciples leaving, and they ran on foot and got there ahead of them. Coming off the boat, Jesus saw the great crowd and had compassion for them because they were like sheep without a shepherd. He taught them many things until late in the day.

The disciples asked Jesus to send the crowd away so they could go to surrounding villages and buy themselves something to eat. But Jesus told His disciples to give them something to eat. The disciples asked if they should go and spend 200 denarii (worth 200 days' wages) on bread and give them something to eat. Jesus asked them how many loaves the disciples had. They reported that a boy in the crowd had five loaves and two fish.

The feeding of the five thousand is the first time the Gospel of John runs parallel with the other three Gospels (John 6:1–13)—A. T. Robertson, *A Harmony of the Gospels*.

Then, Jesus told the crowd to sit on the grass in groups of hundreds and fifties. He took the five loaves and two fish and blessed the food and broke the loaves, and He kept giving them to the disciples; and He divided up the two fish among the five thousand men, plus women and children. The crowd ate and was satisfied. After that they picked up twelve full baskets of leftovers.

Peril at Sea (Mark 6:45–56; Matt. 14:22–36; John 6:14–21)

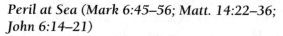

It was now dark, and Jesus told the disciples to get into the boat and go before Him to the other side of the sea and He would send the crowds away. After sending the crowds away, He went to the mountain to pray alone because He knew that some were about to take Him by force to make Him king.

Then strong winds came up at sea, and Jesus saw that the disciples were having a hard time rowing. Sometime between three and six in the morning, Jesus came to them walking on the water. When the disciples saw Him walking on the sea, they were afraid. They thought He was a ghost and cried out in fear. Jesus spoke to them and dispelled their fears.

Peter said to Jesus that if it was really Him, He should allow Peter to come to Him on the water. Jesus invited Peter to come. Peter came out of the boat and walked on the water. Then Peter was distracted by the wind and became afraid and began to sink. Peter cried out for Jesus to save him. Immediately Jesus took hold of Peter with His hand.

Immediately Jesus stretched out His hand and took hold of him, and said to him, "O, you of little faith, why did you doubt?" (Matt. 14:31, NASB).

They got into the boat, and the wind stopped. The disciples in the boat worshiped Jesus and confessed, "You are certainly God's Son!" (Matt. 14:33, NASB).

Crossing over, they came to the land of Gennesaret. The men who lived there recognized Him and brought to Jesus all who were ill from the surrounding district. The sick asked Him just to be able to touch the fringe of His cloak; and as many as touched it were cured.

Jesus said to them, "I am the bread of life; he who comes to Me shall not hunger, and he who believes in Me shall never thirst. But I said to you, that you have seen Me, and yet do not believe. All that the Father gives me shall come to Me, and the one who comes to Me I will certainly not cast out. For I have come down from heaven, not to do My own will, but the will of Him who sent Me" (John 6:35–38, NASB).

The Nature of Messiah (John 6:22–7:1; Mark 7:1–23; Matt. 15:1–20)

The next day in the synagogue in Capernaum, some of the same crowd who had eaten the loaves and fishes left Jesus in disgust when they learned that He is the Bread of life, not a political messiah. Jesus told the crowd not to work for food that perishes but for food that gives eternal life. This comes from the Son of Man because God the Father has put His seal on Him. Jesus told them to believe in Him because He was sent by the Father.

The Jews complained about Jesus because He claimed to be the Bread of life that came from heaven. Jesus answered the Jews and made His claim again. Everyone who would believe in Him would have eternal life.

Many of His disciples thought that this was a hard, difficult saying. Jesus knew that His disciples grumbled at His teaching and asked if this caused them to stumble. Jesus told them that the Spirit, not the flesh, gives life. Jesus knew from the beginning that some would not believe. That is why He said that no one could come to Him unless it was granted him from the Father.

Then the Lord said, "Because this people draw near with their words and honor Me with their lip service, but they remove their hearts far from Me, and their reverence for Me consists of tradition learned by rote, therefore behold, I will once again deal marvelously with this people, wondrously marvelous; and the wisdom of their wise men shall perish, and the discernment of their discerning men will be concealed" (Isa. 29:13–14, NASB).

As a result of this teaching, many of His disciples left Him. Jesus asked if the Twelve wanted to go as well. Peter replied that Jesus had the words of eternal life. Peter affirmed that they believed and that Jesus was the Holy One of God.

Jesus replied that He had chosen them and yet one of them was a devil, referring to Judas Iscariot.

After all of this, Jesus stayed in Galilee and didn't go to Judea because of the growing hostility among the religious leaders who sought to kill Him. A number of the Pharisees and scribes from Jerusalem came to question Him because they had seen some of His disciples eat with defiled, unwashed hands. These Pharisees wanted to know why Jesus' disciples hadn't observed the tradition of the elders. Jesus, quoting Isaiah, replied that the Jews honored God with their lips but their hearts were far from Him.

Jesus claimed that the Pharisees nicely set aside the commandments of God so that they could keep their tradition, and He gave the example of them not caring for their parents. They took what they should have given their parents and declared it a "Corban," a dedication to God (cf. Exod. 21:17 and Lev. 20:9).

Jesus called the crowd to Him and told them to listen and understand. He then told them a parable. There is nothing outside a man that is going into him that can defile him. It is only the things that come out of the man that can defile him.

Corban

Corban comes from the Greek, meaning "an offering," which was used in two ways. It was a Hebrew term related to sacrifices. It was also used to signify a gift given to God (Mark 7:11). The term was basically used to mean any offering given to the Temple.

Jesus Withdraws to Tyre and Sidon (Mark 7:24–30; Matt. 15:21–28)

Jesus went to the region of Tyre and Sidon and entered a house. He didn't want anyone to notice this, but He couldn't escape notice. Hearing He was there, a Gentile women of the Syrophoenician race (Canaanite), who had a daughter with an unclean spirit, immediately came and fell at His feet and asked Jesus repeatedly to cast the demon out.

At first Jesus didn't answer her. Then He told her He was sent to the lost sheep of the house of Israel. But the woman came and worshiped Him and showed spiritual insight and great faith. Jesus said that because of her great faith her daughter would be healed. She found this to be true when she returned home.

Gentile

Gentile comes from the Greek for heathen. For the Jews, it represented one who was not Jewish (synonymous with heathen or pagan) (cf. Matt. 4:15; Rom. 3:29; 11:11, 13; 15:10; 16:4; Gal. 2:8, 12, 14; Eph. 3:1).

Withdrawal for a Third Time (Mark 7:31–8:12; Matt. 15:29–16:4)

Jesus went out of Tyre through Sidon, around to the eastern side of the Sea of Galilee, back into the region of Decapolis. A deaf man who had difficulty speaking was brought to Jesus for healing. Jesus took the man aside and put His fingers into his ears, and after spitting, He touched the man's tongue with the saliva. He then looked up to heaven with a deep sigh and said to the deaf man, "Be opened!" The man could then hear, and he spoke plainly.

But the LORD provided a great fish to swallow Jonah, and Jonah was inside the fish three days and three nights (Jon. 1:17).

At this time another great crowd numbering four thousand (not counting women and children, cf. Matt. 15:38) had been with Him for three days, and He had healed many. Because they had nothing to eat, Jesus had compassion on them and called His disciples and asked how many loaves they had. Answer: seven and a few small fish. Again He commanded them to sit on the ground, and He took the seven loaves and the fish, gave thanks, and shared it with all. They ate and were filled, and seven baskets of broken pieces were collected after eating.

Immediately Jesus and the disciples entered a boat and came to Dalmanutha where He was confronted by a group of Pharisees and Sadducees. They wanted Jesus to show them a sign from heaven. He told them an evil and adulterous generation shall have no sign but the sign of Jonah, and He left them and again went by boat to the other side.

Caesarea Philippi was in the foothills of Mount Hermon. It was a beautiful setting and one that was filled with reminders of pagan worship. Herschel Hobbs said, "This was an ideal setting for the teaching Jesus was to do. In addition to the seclusion which is offered, the very atmosphere was permeated with a fusion of the forces of pagan and Jewish culture and religion and the powers of earthly empires, all of which stood in direct contrast to the kingdom of God, the King, and the revelation of God which He was and taught"—Hobbs, *The Life and Times of Jesus*, 94.

A Blind Man Is Healed in Bethsaida (Mark 8:13–26; Matt. 16:5–12)

Jesus and the disciples crossed the Sea of Galilee and arrived at Bethsaida on their way to Caesarea Philippi. There Jesus healed a blind man. This is the only healing Jesus performed in two stages.

Caesarea Philippi (Mark 8:27–30; Matt. 16:13–20; Luke 9:18–21)

Time had come for a moment of truth with Jesus' disciples. So He took them to Caesarea

Philippi where they could be away from the crowds.

Going forth, Jesus and His disciples went into the villages of Caesarea Philippi. On the way Jesus questioned the disciples with regard to who the people said He was. Some had said John the Baptist, others Elijah or another of the prophets. But Jesus asked them who *they* thought He was.

Peter answered, "Thou art the Christ, the Son of the living God" (Matt. 16:16, KJV). Jesus blessed Peter and responded that flesh and blood had not revealed this to him but the Father in heaven. Jesus went on to tell Peter that His church would be built on the knowledge that He is the Christ and that Peter, and the others, would have the responsibility to teach on earth what the Father has already fixed in heaven. Then Jesus charged them not to tell anyone that He was the Christ.

Jesus' Rejection, Death, Resurrection Foretold (Mark 8:31–37; Matt.16:21–26; Luke 9:22–25)

Jesus began to teach the disciples that He must go to Jerusalem and be rejected by and suffer much at the hands of the elders, chief priests, and scribes and be killed and raised up after three days. Peter reacted strongly to this news and began to rebuke Jesus, for he believed this couldn't happen. But Jesus turned to Peter and rebuked him in the strongest possible way, calling him "Satan" and telling him that he was a "stumbling block" because he had his mind on man's interests and not God's (Matt. 16:23).

Jesus expressly informed the disciples that the nature of discipleship was costly indeed! To follow Jesus would demand that a man should take

Then Jesus said to His disciples, "If any one wishes to come after Me, let him deny himself, and take up his cross and follow Me. For whoever wishes to save his life shall lose it; but whoever loses his life for My sake shall find it. For what will a man be profited, if he gains the whole world, and forfeits his soul?" (Matt. 16:24–26, NASB).

up his cross and deny self to serve Him. For material gain is nothing as compared to God's kingdom and eternal salvation. What does a man have even if he *gained the whole world* and in the process lost his soul?

The Transfiguration (Mark 9:2–8; Matt.17:1–8; Luke 9:28–36)

Several days after Jesus' teaching regarding the Resurrection and the cost of discipleship, He took Peter, James, and John and went up into the mountain to pray. As Jesus prayed, "the appearance of His face became different, and His clothing became white and gleaming" (Luke 9:29, NASB), and Moses and Elijah appeared and talked with Jesus. Having fallen asleep, Peter and the others who were now "fully awake" (v. 32) saw Jesus' glory and Moses and Elijah standing with Him.

Peter, overwhelmed by the experience, suggested building three tabernacles, one each for Jesus, Moses, and Elijah. As Peter spoke, a cloud formed and overshadowed them; and as they entered the cloud, they heard a voice from out of the cloud that said, "This is My beloved Son, with whom I am well-pleased; listen to Him!" (Matt. 17:5, NASB).

Jesus Heals a Boy with Epilepsy (Mark 9:14–50; Matt. 17:14–18:14; Luke 9:37–50)

Still in the region of Caesarea Philippi, Jesus, Peter, James, and John returned to the rest of the disciples and found a large crowd around them and some scribes arguing with them. The crowd ran to greet Jesus. Jesus asked them what they had been discussing. One of the crowd answered that he had brought his son, possessed with a spirit which made him mute, to be healed, but the disciples couldn't heal him.

The Transfiguration of Jesus most probably occurred on Mount Hermon near Caesarea Philippi—A. T. Robertson, *A Harmony of the Gospels*.

Tabernacle

Tabernacle is the rendering of several Greek and Hebrew words which are basically synonyms for dwelling, tent, house, place of sanctity, or temple. The Transfiguration was probably not long before the Feast of Tabernacles (near the end of September) and Peter may have meant that they should celebrate the feast on the mountain instead of going to Jerusalem—A. T. Robertson, *A Harmony of the Gospels*.

Jesus responded: "O unbelieving generation, how long shall I be with you? How long shall I put up with you? Bring him to Me!" (Mark 9:19, NASB). The boy was brought to Him, and he was immediately thrown into convulsion. Jesus asked how long this had been happening. From childhood, the father replied. The father than asked Jesus to heal the boy if it were possible.

And Jesus said to him, "'If You can?' All things are possible to him who believes." Immediately the boy's father cried out and began saying, "I do believe; help my unbelief" (Mark 9:23–24, NASB).

Jesus told the father that all things were possible for those who believe. The father cried out that he did believe and to help him with his unbelief. Jesus rebuked the unclean spirit. The spirit cried out and threw the boy into terrible convulsions and then came out of him. The boy lay so still that some thought him dead. Jesus took him by the hand and raised him.

Going into a house, the disciples wanted to know why they could not cast out the spirit and heal the boy. Jesus replied that it was because they had little faith and that kind comes out only by prayer and fasting.

"For truly I say to you, if you have faith as a mustard seed, you shall say to this mountain, 'Move from here to there,' and it shall move; and nothing shall be impossible to you" (Matt. 17:20, NASB).

Returning quietly through Galilee, Jesus taught the disciples that the Son of Man would be delivered up into the hands of men, that He would die, and be resurrected after three days. Again, they didn't understand but were afraid to ask Him about it.

Jesus Pays the Temple Tax (Matt. 17:24–27)

Having come to Capernaum, the tax collectors came to Peter and asked if his master paid the two-drachma—equivalent of two denarii or two days' wages—as the Temple tax. Peter answered "Yes."

Going into the house, Jesus asked Peter what he thought: Should governments—kings of the earth—collect customs or poll tax from their citizens or from strangers. From strangers, Peter answered. So, replied Jesus, the sons—or citizens—are exempt. But, as not to give offense, Jesus told him to go to the sea and look into the mouth of the first fish caught and he would find a "stater"—or shekel—worth four drachmas. Then he was to take that and give it to the tax collectors for Jesus and Peter.

Who Is the Greatest? (Mark 9:33–37; Matt. 18:1–5; Luke 9:46–48)

The disciples came to Jesus and wanted to know who was the greatest in the kingdom of heaven. Jesus sat down with the Twelve and told them that if any man would be first, he must be last and minister to all.

Jesus Rebukes John's Misplaced Zeal (Mark 9:38–50; Matt. 18:6–14; Luke 9:49–50)

John told Jesus that the disciples had seen a man, not a part of their group, casting out demons in Jesus' name and that they had forbidden the man from doing so. Jesus replied that he who was not against them was for them.

Jesus further told them that if their hand caused them to stumble, they should cut it off. For it was better to face life crippled than to be whole and go to hell. The same is true of an eye.

The shepherd leaves the ninety-nine and goes after the lost one. If the lost one is found, the shepherd rejoices over it more than over the ninety-nine that didn't go astray. Likewise, it is not the Father's will that one of these little ones perish.

How to Treat a Brother Who Has Sinned (Matt. 18:15–35)

Jesus taught the disciples a procedure for restoring a brother or sister who has sinned. Peter asked Jesus how often should a brother who sins against him be forgiven. Seven times? Jesus answered, "Seventy times seven."

Jesus told them the parable of a man who owed his king ten thousand talents. The man couldn't repay the debt. He and his family were about to be sold to cover the debt. But the man pleaded with his king to forgive the entire debt, and the king did.

The king forgave the servant $1,200,000; and the servant refused to forgive $17—A. T. Robertson, *A Harmony of the Gospels.*

Later the servant whose debt had been forgiven went out and found a fellow servant who owed him a hundred denarii, and he seized the one that owed him and began to choke him, demanding repayment. The fellow servant fell down and began to beg him to have patience and he would repay his fellow servant. But, the servant whose own debt the king had forgiven had his fellow servant thrown into prison until he could repay the debt.

Other servants were deeply grieved by what happened and reported this to the king. So the king called the servant, whose debt he had forgiven, to come back. The king called the servant who had been shown mercy, but who refused to show the same, "wicked" and handed him over to be tortured until he should repay all that he owed the king.

Jesus said that is what His heavenly Father would do to them if each one didn't forgive his brother from his heart.

The Cost of Following Jesus
(Matt. 8:19–22; Luke 9:57–62)

A man came to Jesus and said that he would follow Jesus wherever He went. Jesus replied that foxes and birds have homes and places to rest, but the Son of Man had nowhere to lay His

33

But Jesus said to him, "No one, after putting his hand to the plow and looking back, is fit for the kingdom of God" (Luke 9:62, NASB).

head. Others expressed a desire to follow Jesus but said they had other business to take care of before following Him. Jesus clearly expressed the urgency of obedience now.

Jesus Brothers' Counsel, Then to Jerusalem through Samaria (John 7:2–10; Luke 9:51–56)

Jesus was still in Galilee and not willing to go to Judea because the Jews were seeking to kill Him. It was time for the Feast of Tabernacles. Jesus' unbelieving brothers wanted Him to go to Judea to perform miracles, but He rejected their advice. His time hadn't come yet, so He stayed in Galilee.

Later Jesus went quietly, in secret, through Samaria to Jerusalem for the feast.

THE LATER JUDEAN MINISTRY

The Feast of Tabernacles Celebrated (John 7:11–52)

The religious leaders sought Jesus at the feast. The crowds had mixed opinions about Him. But all were silent because they feared the religious leaders. Midway during the feast Jesus went into the Temple and taught. The Jews marveled at His teaching because He didn't have human credentials. Jesus answered and told them that His teaching wasn't His but the One who sent Him.

This ministry lasted about three months in A.D. 29 (or 28 if Jesus' ministry was only two and a half years in length). Also this ministry is recorded with John giving the Jerusalem ministry and Luke that in Judea.—A. T. Robertson, *A Harmony of the Gospels*.

An Adultress Brought to Jesus for Judgment (John 7:53–8:11)

The day after the Feast of Tabernacles ended, Jesus came back to the Temple courts where He taught. While He was teaching, some of the religious leaders brought to Him a woman who had been caught in the act of adultery. They quoted the Law of Moses regarding the penalty for adultery. They asked Jesus what He had to say about this situation.

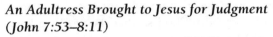

If there is a man who commits adultery with another man's wife, one who commits adultery with his friend's wife, the adulterer and the adulteress shall surely be put to death (Lev. 20:10, NASB; cf. Deut. 22:22–24).

Jesus stooped down to write on the ground while the religious leaders pressed Him for an answer. Jesus then invited those without sin to be the first to carry out the sentence prescribed by Moses' Law. Beginning with the oldest, all of the accusers walked away. Jesus was left face-to-face with the woman, whom He asked, "Where are your accusers?" She responded by addressing Jesus as Lord and acknowledging that there were no longer any accusers. Jesus told her to go and sin no more.

The Light of the World (John 8:12–59)

During the Feast of Tabernacles, the Court of the Women was lighted by candelabra. In this setting, Jesus proclaimed that He was the Light of the world. The Pharisees claimed He was bearing witness to Himself; therefore, His witness was false. Jesus responded that even if He did bear witness to Himself, His witness was true because He knew both where He had come from and where He was going.

Jesus Heals a Blind Man (John 9:1–41)

As Jesus walked in Jerusalem, He passed a beggar, blind from birth. His disciples asked Jesus if it was the blind man's sins or those of his parents that had caused him to be born blind. Jesus answered that neither was the case. That man had been born blind so that the works of God could be shown in him. Jesus went on to say that they must do the works of God as long as it is day, for the night was coming when no man could work. He meant that while He was in the world He was the Light of the world.

After having said this, Jesus spat on the ground, made clay, and applied the clay to the man's eyes. Then He told the man to go wash in the pool of Siloam. The man did so and came back with sight.

The Good Shepherd (John 10:1–21)

In the parable of the good shepherd, Jesus drew a picture of the hostile Pharisees. He indicated that He was going to die for His flock and come to life again. The sheep will know the shepherd's voice, and he will lead them out, but they will flee from a stranger.

Yet the crowd didn't understand Jesus' figure of speech. So He told them more plainly that He

The Pool of Siloam is found three times in the Bible: Nehemiah 3:15, Isaiah 8:6, and John 9:7. The fact that Jesus sent the blind man to wash in the pool indicates that it was near the Temple. It was from Siloam that water was brought in a golden container to the Temple during the Feast of Tabernacles. The pool is fed by a conduit, cut through solid rock for a distance of 1,780 feet, which starts at the Virgin's Spring. It was cut from this source because it is the only spring of fresh water in the immediate neighborhood of Jerusalem.

was the Good Shepherd, the door to salvation. He was the key to an abundant life.

The Mission of the Seventy (Luke 10:1–24)

Jesus now appointed seventy others and sent them out by twos to every city and place in advance of His arrival. He told them of the plentiful harvest and the real shortage of workers. He told them to plead to the Lord of the harvest for workers.

Jesus told them that they were sent out as lambs in the middle of wolves. They were not to take any extra things and to greet no one on the way. When they first entered a house, they were to say, "Peace be to this house" (Luke 10:5, NASB). If a man of peace lived there, he would acknowledge their blessing. Then they should stay in that house and eat and drink what they were given "for the laborer is worthy of his wages" (Luke 10:7, NASB); and they weren't to keep moving from house to house.

Likewise with cities: If they were received, they were to eat what was set before them. They were to heal those who were sick and to tell them that the kingdom of God had come near to them. If, on the other hand, a city didn't receive them, they should leave and wipe off even the dust of the place that clings to their feet. Yet they should be sure of this: that the kingdom of God had come near. In fact, Jesus told them that it would be more tolerable in the end for Sodom than for the cities that didn't receive them: Chorazin, Bethsaida, and Capernaum.

The person who listened to them was listening to Jesus, and the one who rejected them was rejecting Jesus and the One who sent Him!

"Truly, truly, I say to you, I am the door of the sheep. . . . I am the door; if anyone enters through Me, he shall be saved, . . . I came that they might have life, and might have it abundantly. I am the good shepherd; the good shepherd lays down His life for the sheep" (John 10:7, 9–11, NASB).

And He was saying to them, "The harvest is plentiful, but the laborers are few; therefore beseech the Lord of the harvest to send out laborers into His harvest" (Luke 10:2, NASB).

The seventy returned with joy and reported that even the demons obeyed them in Jesus' name. Jesus responded that He was watching Satan fall from heaven like lightning and that He had given them authority to step on serpents and scorpions and power over the enemy so that nothing could injure them.

At that moment Jesus rejoiced greatly in the Holy Spirit and spoke to the Father and praised Him who is Lord of heaven and earth. He thanked the Father for hiding these things from the wise and revealing them to babes, for it was pleasing to God.

Jesus said that the Father had handed all things over to Him and that no one knew who the Son was except the Father and who the Father was except the Son and anyone to whom the Son willed to reveal Him.

Turning to the disciples, Jesus told them that the eyes that saw what they had seen were blessed because many prophets and kings had wished to see and hear what they had but did not.

"Hear, O Israel! The LORD is our God, the LORD is one! And you shall love the LORD your God with all your heart and with all your soul and with all your might. And these words, which I am commanding you today, shall be on your heart" (Deut. 6:4–6, NASB).

Jesus Answers a Lawyer's Question About Eternal Life (Luke 10:25–37)

A lawyer put Jesus to the test and asked a question about eternal life. He addressed Jesus as "Teacher" and wanted to know what he had to do to inherit eternal life. Jesus asked the lawyer how the Law read to him. The lawyer answered by quoting Deuteronomy 6:5 and adding to love God "with all your mind" and to love "your neighbor as yourself" (Lev. 19:18).

Jesus told the lawyer that he had answered correctly and that if he did this he would live. But the lawyer, wanting to justify himself, asked

Jesus just who his neighbor was. Jesus responded with the story of a good Samaritan.

A man traveling from Jerusalem to Jericho was robbed, stripped of his clothing, beaten, and left half dead. Just by chance a Jewish priest was also going down the road; but when he saw the beaten man, he walked on the other side. A Levite also walked to the other side when he saw the man.

Then followed a Samaritan who saw the man and felt compassion and went to him and bandaged his wounds, poured oil and wine on them, carried the man to an inn, and took care of him. The next day the Samaritan gave two denarii to the innkeeper and told him to care for the injured man, and if it cost more, he would return and pay him the extra.

Jesus asked which of the three proved to be a neighbor to the injured man. The lawyer answered that it was the man who showed mercy. Jesus told the lawyer to go and do the same.

A Guest of Mary and Martha (Luke 10:38–42)

In Bethany near Jerusalem, Jesus was the guest in the home of Mary and Martha. Mary sat at Jesus' feet to listen to the words He taught. Martha, however, was distracted with all her preparations, and she went to Jesus and asked Him if He cared that Mary had left her to do all the serving alone. Martha even asked Jesus to tell her sister to help her.

But Martha didn't get the response she was expecting. Instead, Jesus told Martha that she was worried and bothered about so many things, but only a few things were really important, that is, "necessary"—really only one, in

Levite comes from the Hebrew word meaning "sons of Levi." Besides referring to all descendants of Levi (Exod. 6:25; Lev. 25:32; Josh. 21:3, 41), it was also the distinctive title of that portion of the tribe set apart for the service of the sanctuary and subordinate to the priests (Num. 8:6; Ezra 2:70; John 1:19). We sometimes read of "the Levitical priests" (cf. Josh. 3:3).

There was another Bethany beyond Jordan (John 1:28). Jesus was in Bethany near Jerusalem again (John 12:1–8). It was His Jerusalem home in the early days of Passion Week, the week before the Crucifixion.

fact. Mary had chosen the important thing, and that would not be taken away from her.

Jesus Instructs His Disciples on Prayer (Luke 11:1–13)

Jesus was praying, and when He stopped, one of the disciples asked Him to teach them to pray because John had taught His disciples to pray. Jesus responded with what has long been called the "Lord's Prayer" or the "Model Prayer" (Luke 11:2–4).

He said to them, "Whenever you pray, say: Father, Your name be honored as holy. Your kingdom come. Give us each day our daily bread. And forgive us our sins, for we ourselves also forgive everyone in debt to us. And do not bring us into temptation" (Luke 11:1–4, HCSB).

Jesus taught them further. What if one of them had a friend and went to him at midnight and asked him to lend three loaves of bread because he had received a traveling friend and had nothing to feed this other friend. His friend told him from behind his locked door that he and his children were already in bed and he wasn't going to get out of bed to give him anything. The friend was told not to bother him and to go away! But he persisted, and finally the friend got up and gave as much as was needed. Jesus then taught them the importance of persistence in prayer.

"So I say to you, keep asking, and it will be given to you. Keep searching, and you will find. Keep knocking, and the door will be opened to you. For everyone who asks receives, and the one who searches finds, and to the one who knocks, the door will be opened" (Luke 11:9–10, HCSB).

What if one of the fathers in the group had been asked for a fish by his son? Would he have given his son a snake instead? If evil men know how to give good things to their children, just think how much more the heavenly Father gives the Holy Spirit to those who ask Him!

Jesus Heals a Man Who Is Mute (Luke 11:14–36)

Jesus cast a demon out of a man who had been made mute by it. When the demon left, the man spoke, and the crowds marveled. Some of the crowd said that Jesus cast out demons by Beelzebub, the ruler of demons. But Jesus reminded them that a house or kingdom divided against itself cannot stand. Satan will not cast out Satan (cf. Mark 3:19–30 and Matt. 12:22–37.)

Jesus cast out demons by the finger of God, and the kingdom of God had come upon them. One of the women in the crowd shouted that the womb that bore Him and the breasts that nursed Him were blessed. Jesus responded, "On the contrary, blessed are those who hear the word of God, and observe it" (Luke 11:28, NASB).

Again the crowds gathered and Jesus stated that this generation was an evil one which sought a sign but that none would be given except the sign of Jonah (Jon. 3:1–4). Just as Jonah was a sign to the Ninevites, so the Son of Man was a sign to that generation.

The Queen of the South, or the Queen of Sheba (1 Kings 10), came from the uttermost ends of the earth and spared no expense in order to listen to the wisdom of Solomon, and she believed the report she had heard of him.

The Queen of the South believed in the wisdom of Solomon, but most of the Jews rejected the far greater wisdom of Jesus. The men on Nineveh repented at the preaching of Jonah, but the majority of the Jews didn't realize that they were witnessing something far greater in Jesus. Thus, the Queen of the South and the men of Nineveh will stand up and condemn that generation.

Breakfast with a Pharisee (Luke 11:37–54)

As Jesus was speaking, a Pharisee asked Him to breakfast, and He went to eat with him. When the Pharisee saw that Jesus hadn't first ceremonially washed before the meal, he was surprised. But Jesus said to him that the Pharisees cleaned the outside of the cup and the platter, while their insides were full of robbery and wickedness. Jesus called them "foolish" because He who made the outside also made the inside.

Beware of Greed (Luke 12)

In the meantime, a crowd of so many thousands had gathered that they were stepping on one another. Jesus started speaking to the disciples first that they should beware of the hypocritical deeds of the Pharisees. Eventually all deeds and words would be uncovered and revealed. He told them not to be afraid of those who kill the body, for that is all they can do. Jesus warned them instead to fear the One who, after He has killed, has authority to cast into hell. He was the One to fear! Even relatively insignificant sparrows—five are sold for two cents—not one of them was forgotten by God. Even the very hairs on the disciples heads were numbered. They were more valuable than many sparrows.

Then Jesus told them a parable about a certain rich man whose land was fruitful, so productive that the rich man couldn't store all his crops.

"Beware, and be on your guard against every form of greed; for not even when one has an abundance does his life consist of his possessions. . . .' You fool! This very night your soul is required of you. . . .' So is the man who lays up treasure for himself, and is not rich toward God" (Luke 12:15, 20–21, NASB).

The rich man reasoned that he should tear down his barns and build larger ones to store all his grain and goods. Then the rich man told himself that he had many goods laid up for many years to come, so he should take it easy, eat, drink, and be merry.

But God told the rich man that he was a fool. His life would be taken—his soul would be required of him—that very night. Who will then own all that the rich man has prepared? The man who hordes treasure for himself and is not rich toward God will lose his very soul.

"But if God so arrays the grass in the field, which is alive today and tomorrow is thrown into the furnace, how much more will He clothe you, O men of little faith!" (Luke 12:28, NASB).

This was the reason Jesus told His disciples not to be anxious about their lives, about what they were to eat or what clothes they were to wear. "For life is more than food, and the body more than clothing" (Luke 12:23, NASB).

Call to Repent (Luke 13:1–9)

On the same occasion some of the crowd told Jesus about Galileans whose blood Pilate shed with their sacrifices. Jesus asked them if they supposed these Galileans were greater sinners than all other Galileans because they suffered that fate. No, answered Jesus. Everyone must repent or perish.

Jesus asked those present if they supposed that the eighteen on whom the tower in Siloam fell and were killed were worse culprits than all the men who lived in Jerusalem. No, answered Jesus. All must repent or likewise perish.

Healing on the Sabbath (Luke 13:10–21)

Present that day was a woman who had been bent double, who could not straighten up at all for eighteen years as the result of a sickness caused by a spirit. Jesus saw her, called her over, and told her she was free from her sickness. He then laid His hands on her, and immediately she was able to stand straight again, and she began glorifying God.

The synagogue official, angered because Jesus had healed on the Sabbath, told the crowds there were six days during which work should be done, that they should come during one of the six and get healed, but not on the Sabbath day.

Jesus answered the official by calling him a hypocrite because he also did work on the Sabbath but he wouldn't allow a daughter of Abraham bound for eighteen long years to be healed on the Sabbath. The people were pleased with what Jesus said, but His enemies were humiliated.

Sabbath

Sabbath is from the Hebrew and Greek, meaning "to rest from labor." In the Old Testament the seventh day of the week (Saturday) was the day of worship and rest for the Jews (Exod. 20:8–11). The Sabbath is different from the Christian Sunday, though the two are often confused. The Christian Sunday, also known as the Lord's Day, is the first day of the week and is observed to acknowledge the Resurrection of Jesus.

The Feast of Dedication in Jerusalem (Hanukkah) (John 10:22–39)

At the Feast of Dedication, Jesus was walking in the Temple in Solomon's porch. The Jews came around Him and asked Him how long He was going to keep them in suspense. They demanded that He tell them plainly if He was the Christ.

Jesus answered that He had told them and they hadn't believed. The works He did in His Father's name bore witness of Him. He further told them that because they hadn't believed they were not His sheep, because His sheep hear His voice and He knows them and they follow Him. He will give them eternal life, and they shall never perish, and no one shall snatch them out of His hand.

The Feast of Dedication or Hanukkah lasted eight days in December. Josephus called it the Feast of Lights because a candle was lighted each day until a total of eight was reached. This feast commemorated the victories of Judas Maccabeus in 167 B.C. and the reinstitution of Temple worship.

THE LATER PEREAN MINISTRY

Jesus Teaches and Heals in Perea
(John 10:40–42; Luke 13:22–14:24)

Jesus went away again beyond the Jordan to the place where John was first baptizing and stayed there. Many came to Him and said that while John performed no sign, everything John had said about Jesus was true, and many believed in Him.

Jesus went through the cities and villages teaching and traveling toward Jerusalem. Someone asked Him if only a few were being saved. Jesus answered that they should strive to enter by the narrow door; for many will seek to enter and won't be able.

Jesus told them that just because He had been among them, they wouldn't automatically be a part of the kingdom of God. Those in the kingdom would come from east, west, north, and south. Many who were first would be last.

Counting the Cost of Discipleship
(Luke 14:25–35)

Large crowds followed Jesus, and He warned them to count the cost of being His disciples. Jesus said that if anyone came to Him and didn't hate his own father, mother, wife, children, brothers and sisters, even his own life, that one couldn't be His disciple. Whoever didn't carry his own cross and come after Jesus couldn't be His disciple.

Parables of the Lost Sheep, the Lost Coin, and the Lost Son (Luke 15:1–32)

While the publicans and sinners drew near Jesus, the Pharisees and scribes murmured

This period probably takes place from the Feast of Dedication in A.D. 29 to the last journey in A.D. 30, about three and a half months. The period of three to four months from dedication to the final Passover is divided by another visit to Jerusalem. We can't tell how many weeks preceded this event. We should be reminded that all along here we have only a few examples of Jesus' teaching and works.

against Jesus for associating with the sinners. So Jesus told them three parables that show God's love for the lost.

Three Parables on Stewardship (Luke 16:1–17:10)

Jesus told the disciples of a certain rich man who had a steward who was reported to him as having wasted his master's assets. The rich man called in his steward and asked for an accounting.

The steward wondered what he could do since his master was taking his stewardship away, for he was too weak to dig and ashamed to beg. He came up with a plan so that when he was removed from his office, others would be grateful to him and receive him into their homes.

He called in each one of his master's debtors and reduced what they owed to his master. They were happy with being able to settle their debt for less than what it was.

The rich "master praised the unrighteous steward because he had acted shrewdly; for the sons of this age are more shrewd in relation to their own kind than the sons of light" (Luke 16:8, NASB).

Jesus said that those who are faithful in small things will be faithful with much. Those who are faithful with worldly goods can be trusted with true riches.

The Pharisees, who were lovers of money, were listening to all this; and they scoffed at Him. Jesus replied that they were the ones who justified themselves in the sight of men, but God knew their hearts; "for that which is highly esteemed among men is detestable in the sight of God" (Luke 16:15, NASB). The Law and the Prophets were proclaimed until John, but since then, the gospel of the kingdom of God has been preached.

Mammon of unrighteousness

The parable referred to material possessions, not just to money. Generalized under the comparison of the "mammon of unrighteousness," Jesus added these words as an express command in connection with the right use of material things. But His followers are to be so free from the low, selfish, and covetous motives that dominated the world of the unjust steward that they will use the worldly goods entrusted to them by the Father in a manner that will bring blessings to others and be conducive to their own eternal welfare.

"No servant can serve two masters; for either he will hate the one, and love the other, or else he will hold to one, and despise the other. You cannot serve God and mammon" (Luke 16:13, NASB).

Jesus contrasted a wealthy man who had everything he wanted with a poor beggar named Lazarus, whose body was covered with sores. Lazarus was laid at the rich man's gate and fed on the crumbs that fell from the rich man's table.

Both men died. Jesus showed how their conditions were reversed in the world to come. Lazarus went to heaven, and the rich man found himself tormented in Hades. The rich man asked Abraham to send Lazarus to bring just a drop of water to him to cool his tongue.

But Abraham called the once rich man "child," and reminded him how in life he received his good things and Lazarus bad things; but now their roles were reversed. Besides, between them was a great chasm, which no one from either side could cross.

The former rich man then begged Abraham to send Lazarus to his father's house, for he had five brothers he wanted to warn so they wouldn't end up as he had in the place of torment. But Abraham replied that the brothers have the Scriptures to show them how to avoid Hades.

The rich man then told Father Abraham that if someone went to them from the dead, his brothers would repent! Abraham answered that if they didn't listen to the Scripture they wouldn't be persuaded even if someone rose from the dead.

"It would be better for him if a millstone were hung around his neck and he were thrown into the sea, than that he should cause one of these little ones to stumble" (Luke 17:2, NASB).

At this time Jesus told His disciples that it was inevitable that stumbling blocks would come, but woe to him through whom they came!

Jesus told them to be on guard! If their brother sins, rebuke him. If he repents, forgive him; even if he sins against you seven times a day and

Jesus was apparently at a distance of two or three days' journey (John 11:6, 17) from Bethany; he was probably in Perea. This visit to Bethany, a suburb of Jerusalem ("about two miles from Jerusalem," Luke 11:18, NASB), may be that to which Luke pointed in 13:22.

Jesus said to her, "I am the resurrection and the life; he who believes in Me shall live even if he dies, and everyone who lives and believes in Me shall never die" (John 11:25–26, NASB).

returns to you seven times saying that he repents, forgive him.

Jesus Raises Lazarus from the Dead (John 11:1–54)

While Jesus was in Perea, his friends, Mary and Martha of Bethany, sent word to Him that their brother, Lazarus, was critically ill.

When Jesus got the message, He responded that Lazarus' sickness wasn't to "end in death" (v. 4) but was for God's glory so that the Son of God could be glorified by it. The text plainly states that Jesus loved Martha, her sister, and Lazarus. But after Jesus heard that Lazarus was sick, He stayed where He was two days longer.

When Jesus arrived in Bethany, He found Lazarus already in the tomb for four days. Many Jews were there, consoling Martha and Mary because of the death.

Martha heard that Jesus was coming, so she went to meet Him. Mary stayed in the house. Martha told Jesus that if He had been there, her brother wouldn't have died. She further stated that she believed even then that whatever Jesus asked of God, God would give Him. Jesus told Martha that her brother would rise again. Martha replied that she knew Lazarus would rise again in the resurrection on the last day.

Jesus told Martha that He was the resurrection and the life and asked her if she believed this. She said that she believed He was the Christ, the Son of God.

Martha went to her sister, Mary, and told her secretly that the Teacher was there and was calling for her. Mary got up quickly and went to Jesus who was still at the place where Martha had met Him outside the village. The Jews who were in the house consoling Mary got up and followed her, assuming she was going to the tomb to weep.

Mary came to Jesus and fell at His feet and called Him "Lord." She told Him that if He had been there, her brother wouldn't have died. Jesus saw her and the Jews who came with her weeping. He was deeply moved in spirit and was troubled. He asked them where they had laid Lazarus. They told Him to come and see.

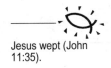

Jesus wept (John 11:35).

The Jews commented on how much Jesus loved Lazarus. But then some of them, remembering that Jesus had given sight to a blind man, asked if He couldn't have kept Lazarus from dying.

Jesus again was deeply moved and came to the tomb (cave) which had a stone lying in front of the entrance. He told them to remove the stone. Martha reminded Jesus that by that time there would be a stench, for he had been dead four days. Jesus reminded her that He had told her if she believed she would see the glory of God.

Sanhedrin means a "council" or "assembly session." This was the great council of the Hebrews. Though the rabbis attempted to trace its origin to the college of seventy elders named by Moses, the first time it was mentioned was during the time of Antiochus the Great, 223–187 B.C. In Jesus' day the Sanhedrin was frequently mentioned as the supreme Jewish court of justice. According to the Mishnah it had seventy members (cf. John 18:22; Mark 14:65).

The stone was removed, and Jesus raised His eyes and spoke to the Father, thanking the Father for hearing Him. He knew that the Father always heard Him; but because of the people standing around, Jesus said this so that they could believe that the Father had sent Jesus.

Having said this, Jesus cried out in a loud voice for Lazarus to come forth, and he did. Lazarus was still bound hand and foot with strips of cloth, and his face wrapped in cloth. Jesus told them to unbind Lazarus and let him go.

This raising of Lazarus set in motion a consultation among the members of the Sanhedrin about what they should do with Jesus. They were afraid He would upset the balance of power and the Romans would take advantage of their loss of power.

Caiaphas, the high priest that year, told them that it would be expedient for them if one man died for the people rather than the whole nation perish. Thus, from that day they planned to kill Him.

The Last Journey to Jerusalem by Way of Samaria and Galilee (Luke 17:11–37)

As Jesus was on His way to Jerusalem through Samaria and Galilee, He entered a certain village where ten leprous men met Him but stood at a distance. They shouted, calling Jesus "Master," and asked Him to have mercy on them. Jesus told them to go and show themselves to the priests; and as they went; they were healed of their disease.

One of them, seeing that he was healed, turned back, glorifying God with a loud voice. He fell on his face at Jesus' feet, giving Him thanks. Jesus said to the man, a Samaritan: "Were there not ten cleansed? But the nine—where are they?" (Luke 17:17, NASB). Jesus told the one to rise and go his way; his faith had made him well.

Going from Galilee through Perea (Mark 10:1–12; Matt. 19:1–12)

When a man takes a wife and marries her, and it happens that she finds no favor in his eyes because he has found some indecency in her, and he writes her a certificate of divorce and puts it in her hand and sends her out from his house (Deut. 24:1, NASB).

Jesus went to the borders of Judea beyond Jordan. Large crowds came to Him again, and He taught them. Pharisees came to Him to test Him and asked if it was lawful for a man to divorce his wife. Jesus asked them what Moses had commanded.

They responded that Moses permitted a man to write a certificate of divorce and send his wife away. But Jesus told them that Moses allowed this because of the hardness of their hearts.

From the beginning of Creation, God's intention was that marriage should be for a lifetime.

Later in the house, the disciples began questioning Him about divorce again. In Matthew 19:9–10, Jesus told His audience that whoever divorced his wife, except for fornication, and married another, commits adultery as does the one who marries the woman who has been divorced. Then the disciples responded to Jesus that if such is the relationship between a man and a woman it was better not to marry."

Eunuch is Greek, literally meaning "bed keeper," or one who has charge of beds and bedchambers. The original Hebrew clearly implied the incapacity that results from mutilation or castration.

Jesus told them that not all men could accept that statement but only those to whom it has been given. Some eunuchs were born from their mothers womb as such; some were made eunuchs by men; and some made themselves eunuchs for the sake of the kingdom of heaven. Jesus told them that the one who is able to accept this, let him do so.

Christ and Children (Mark 10:13–16; Matt. 19:13–15; Luke 18:15–17)

People brought their little children and babies to Jesus to have Him touch them. But the disciples scolded the people. When Jesus saw this, He was angered, and He told the disciples not to forbid them, for the kingdom of God belongs to such as these.

But Jesus said, "Let the children alone, and do not hinder them from coming to Me; for the kingdom of heaven belongs to such as these" (Matt. 19:14, NASB).

Jesus went on to tell them that whosoever will not receive the kingdom of God as a little child will in no way enter into it, and He took them in His arms, blessed them, laid His hands on them, and then left that place.

The Rich Young Ruler and the Parable of the Vineyard (Mark 10:17–31; Matt. 19:16–20:16; Luke 18:18–30)

As He was leaving, a ruler ran to Jesus and kneeled and asked, calling Him "Good teacher," what he had to do to inherit eternal life. Jesus asked the man why he called Him good when none is good but God. Then Jesus asked the young man if he knew and kept the commandments (cf. Exod. 20:12–16; Deut. 5:16–20). The young man asked which ones. Jesus reviewed with him the well-known commandments.

Then Jesus said to his disciples, "I tell you the truth, it is hard for a rich man to enter the kingdom of heaven" (Matt. 19:23).

The young man replied that he had kept all these and wanted to know what he still lacked. Jesus told him that if he wished to be complete, he should sell his possessions, give to the poor, and then he would have treasure in heaven, and to come and follow Him. When the young man heard Jesus, he went away sad because he was wealthy.

Jesus told His disciples it was hard for those who trust in riches to enter God's kingdom. He said it was easier for a camel to go through the eye of a needle than for a rich man to enter God's kingdom. When the disciples heard this, they were astonished and asked who could be saved. Jesus said that with man it was impossible but with God all things are possible.

Peter reminded Jesus that they had left all and followed Him. He asked what they were going to get out of it. Jesus assured Peter that they would be rewarded. But Jesus added that rewards would not be made according to human standards. Many who are first will be last and the last first.

Parable of the Laborers in the Vineyard (Matt. 20:1–16)

Jesus said that the kingdom of heaven was like a landowner who went out early to hire laborers for his vineyard. He agreed to pay them a denarius for the day and sent them into his vineyard. About nine A.M. the landowner went out again, and he saw others standing idle in the marketplace. He told them to go into the vineyard and he would give them whatever was right, so they went. He went out at noon and three P.M. and did the same thing. At about five P.M. he went out and found others standing and asked them why they had been standing idle all day long. They responded that no one had hired them. He told them to go into the vineyard.

When the evening came, the owner told his foreman to call the labors and pay them, beginning with the last group hired to the first. The group hired about five P.M. received a denarius per man. When the group first hired came, they thought they would receive more, but they also each received a denarius. They complained to the landowner that the last group had worked only one hour and they received equal pay to the ones who had "borne the burden and the scorching heat of the day" (v. 12, NASB).

The landowner replied that he was doing them no wrong, for they agreed to work for a denarius a day. The landowner told them further that it was lawful for him to do what he wished with what was his own. He asked the first group if their eyes were envious because he had been generous. Thus the last shall be first, and the first last.

A denarius was a Roman silver coin whose name originally came from its being equal to ten "donkeys" (later increased to sixteen). It was the daily wage of a laborer. In 1922, a denarius was estimated to be worth about seventeen cents. The only way to compute the value of a denarius in our day is to consider what a laborer might earn per day in today's economy.—A. T. Robertson, *A Harmony of the Gospels.*

Death and Resurrection Foretold Again (Mark 10:32–45; Matt. 20:17–28; Luke 18:31–34)

As Jesus was about to go up to Jerusalem, He took the twelve disciples aside and told them that they were going to Jerusalem and that the Son of Man would be delivered to the chief priests and scribes. They would condemn Him to death, deliver Him up to the Gentiles to mock and scourge, and then crucify Him. On the third day He would be raised from the dead.

James and John came up to Him (Matthew records that their mother was with them and made the request, v. 20), and they asked the Master to do for them whatever they asked. Jesus asked what they wanted Him to do. They responded that they wanted Him to grant that they sit one on His right hand and one on His left hand in His glory.

Jesus told them that they didn't know what they had asked. He wanted to know if they were able to go through what He was about to go through. They said that they were. Jesus responded that they would drink the cup He would drink and they would be baptized with the baptism He would receive but it was not His to give with regard to whether they sit on His right or left.

"Whoever wishes to become great among you shall be your servant; and whoever wishes to be first among you shall be slave of all" (Mark 10:43–44, NASB).

When the other ten disciples heard this, they resented James and John's trying to secure the best places in the kingdom.

Jesus reminded them that even He did not come to be served but to serve and to give His life as a ransom for many.

Blind Bartimaeus and His Companion Healed (Mark 10:46–52; Matt. 20:29–34; Luke 18:35–43)

Coming to Jericho with the disciples and a great crowd, Bartimaeus who was a blind beggar, the son of Timaeus, and another blind companion were sitting there by the roadside. Hearing that Jesus of Nazareth was passing by, they began yelling and asked Jesus, son of David, to have mercy on them. Many in the crowd reprimanded the blind men and told them to be silent. But they cried out even more, asking Jesus to have mercy on them.

Jesus stopped, called them, and asked them what they would have Him do. They replied that they wanted to see. Moved with compassion, Jesus touched their eyes and straightway they could see, and they followed Him.

Jesus Visits Zacchaeus (Luke 19:1–9)

As Jesus passed through Jericho, a rich chief tax gatherer named Zacchaeus tried to see Jesus but couldn't because he was short and the crowd was large. So Zacchaeus ran ahead of the crowd and climbed up a sycamore tree so that he could see Jesus, who was about to pass that way. When Jesus got to the tree, He looked up and told Zacchaeus to hurry down because today He must stay at his house. Zacchaeus came down quickly and was glad to receive Jesus. But when the crowd saw this, they began to grumble because Jesus had gone to be the guest of a sinner.

Zacchaeus, who was thankful indeed, told Jesus that he was going to give half his possessions to the poor; and further, if he had ever cheated anyone of anything, he would give back four times as much. Jesus told Zacchaeus

Matthew mentions two blind men, and Mark and Luke describe one, probably the more noticeable one. About the discrepancy as to place, whether Jesus was leaving or was coming near to Jericho, is best explained by the suggestion that the healing occurred after He left the old Jericho, and as He was approaching the new Jericho, which Herod the Great had built some distance away. An older and also possible explanation was that the blind men made petition when He was approaching the city but were not then healed, and only when Jesus had left the city were healed (cf. Mark 8:22–26)—A. T. Robertson, *A Harmony of the Gospels.*

that salvation had come to his house because he, too, was a son of Abraham.

Parable of the Pounds (Luke 19:10–28)

As they were listening, Jesus went on to tell them a parable because, being near Jerusalem, they thought that the kingdom of God was going to appear immediately.

Having spoken, Jesus went on toward Jerusalem.

THE LAST PUBLIC MINISTRY IN JERUSALEM

Jesus Arrives in Bethany and Makes His Triumphal Entry into Jerusalem (John 11:55–12:1, 9–19; Mark 11:1–11; Matt. 21:1–11, 14–17; Luke 19:29–44)

Jesus arrived at Bethany, near Jerusalem, on Friday afternoon. The Jewish Passover was at hand.

As Jesus and His disciples approached Jerusalem, at Bethphage and Bethany, near the Mount of Olives, Jesus sent two disciples to the village. He told them that immediately as they entered, they would find a colt, on which no one had ever sat, tied up. They were to bring it to Jesus.

When they brought the colt they put their clothes on it, and Jesus entered Jerusalem riding the colt.

Many in the crowd spread their garments on the path. Others spread leafy branches they had cut from the fields. The crowd went ahead, shouting, "Hosanna! Blessed is He who comes in the name of the Lord; Blessed is the coming kingdom of our father David; Hosanna in the highest" (Matt. 21:9; cf. Ps. 118:26).

Some of the Pharisees from the crowd asked Jesus to reprimand His disciples. But Jesus said that if they held their peace the stones would cry out.

As Jesus approached the city, He cried over it and foretold of the destruction of the great city.

The blind and the lame came to Him in the Temple, and Jesus healed them. But when the chief priests and the scribes saw the wonderful

This occurred on Friday before Tuesday of Passion Week, spring of A.D. 30 (or A.D. 29 if the feast of John 5:1 was a Passover). If Jesus' ministry lasted over three years, then His death was most likely in A.D. 30, otherwise, in A.D. 29.

Rejoice greatly, O daughter of Zion! Shout in triumph, O daughter of Jerusalem! Behold, your king is coming to you; He is just and endowed with salvation, humble, and mounted on a donkey, even on a colt, the foal of a donkey (Zech. 9:9, NASB).

things that Jesus did and heard the children crying in the Temple, "Hosanna to the Son of David" (v. 14), they were outraged. They asked Jesus if He heard what the crowd was saying. Jesus replied, "Yes; have you never read, 'Out of the mouth of infants and nursing babes Thou hast prepared praise for Thyself?'" (Matt. 21:16, NASB).

That evening, Jesus returned to Bethany from Jerusalem.

The Barren Fig Tree Cursed and the Second Cleansing of the Temple (Mark 11:12–18; Matt. 21:12–13, 18–19; Luke 19:45–48)

The next day, Monday, when they had come out of Bethany and returned to Jerusalem, Jesus was hungry, and He saw at a distance a fig tree in leaf. Jesus went to see if He could find anything on it; but He found nothing but leaves, for it wasn't the season for figs.

His disciples were listening and heard Jesus say to the tree: "May no one ever eat fruit from you again" (Mark 11:14).

Coming to Jerusalem, Jesus entered the Temple and threw out those buying and selling in the Temple and overturned the tables of the money-changers and the seats of those selling doves. Jesus wouldn't allow anyone to carry goods through the Temple.

The chief priests and the scribes heard Jesus and now sought to destroy Him. They were afraid of Him because the crowd was astonished at His teaching.

Greeks Want to See Jesus (John 12:20–50)

A number of Greeks were going up to worship at the feast, and they came to Philip, from Bethsaida of Galilee, and asked him if they could see Jesus. Philip told Andrew, and they told Jesus.

Jesus answered them by telling them that the hour had come for the Son of Man to be glorified. Unless a grain of wheat falls into the earth and dies, it remains alone; but if it dies, it will bear much fruit.

The Barren Fig Tree Withered (Mark 11:19–25; Matt. 21:19–22; Luke 21:37–38)

Every evening Jesus went out of the city. On Tuesday, as they passed by in the morning on their way from Bethany to Jerusalem, they saw the fig tree withered away from the roots. Peter remembered what Jesus had said to the tree and told the Teacher to look, the fig tree He had cursed had withered away.

Jesus told them to have faith in God for truly if one of faith says to the mountain be taken up and thrown into the sea and doesn't doubt in his heart but believes that what he says is going to happen, it will be granted him.

Jesus also told them that whenever they stood praying to forgive if they had anything against anyone so that the Father in heaven would also forgive their sins. But if they don't forgive, the Father in heaven would not forgive their sins.

Jesus' Authority Questioned (Mark 11:27–33; Matt. 21:23–27; Luke 20:1–8)

In the court of the Temple on Tuesday, the Sanhedrin formally challenged the authority of Jesus as an accredited teacher or rabbi. As He walked in the Temple, the chief priests, scribes, and elders came to Jesus and asked Him by what authority He did what He did.

Jesus replied that He would ask them one question, and if they answered Him, He would tell

The Gospels of Matthew, Mark, and Luke give more details of the teaching of Jesus on this Tuesday in the Temple and on the Mount of Olives than for any other single day.

"Therefore, I tell you, all the things you pray and ask for—believe that you have received them, and you will have them" (Mark 11:24, HCSB).

them His authority. The one question was whether the baptism of John was from heaven or from men. The rulers realized they were in a jam, for if they answered "from heaven," Jesus would ask why they hadn't believed Him. But if they said "from men," they feared the people, for all considered John to have been a prophet.

The rulers answered that they didn't know. When they answered that way, Jesus told them that He wouldn't tell them from what authority He did the things He did.

Parable of the Two Sons (Matt. 21:28–32)

Then Jesus asked the Jewish rulers what they thought. He told them about a man who had two sons. The man went to the first son and told him to go work in the vineyard. The son refused to go, but later the son repented and went to work. Then the man went to his second son and also told him to go work in the vineyard. The second son said, "I will, sir," and then didn't go.

Jesus asked the Jewish rulers which son did his father's will. They answered it was the first.

Parable of the Wicked Husbandmen
(Mark 12:1–9; Matt. 21:33–46; Luke 20:9–19)

Then Jesus told them another parable. A landowner planted a vineyard, put a hedge around it, and dug a winepress in it. He built a tower and rented it out to vine growers and went on a journey. When the harvest season came, he sent his servants to the vine growers to receive his produce. They beat one of his servants, killed another, and stoned a third. This time the landowner sent a larger group of servants, and the vine growers did the same thing to them.

Finally the landowner sent his son, believing they would respect his son. But seeing the son, the vine growers realized that here was the heir and that if they killed him they could steal his inheritance. So they threw the son out of the vineyard and killed him.

Parable of the Marriage Feast of the King's Son (Matt. 22:1–14)

Jesus spoke again to them in a parable. The kingdom of heaven could be compared to a king who gave a wedding feast for his son. The king sent out his servants to call those who had been invited to the feast, but they wouldn't come. So the king sent out other servants to tell those who had been invited that he had prepared the dinner. But the ones who had been invited paid no attention and went their own ways. Some others seized the kings' servants, mistreated, and finally killed them. The king was enraged and sent his armies and destroyed the murderers and burned their city.

Then he informed his servants that the wedding was ready but those who were invited were not worthy. He told the servants to go to the main highways and invite everyone they found to the wedding. The servants gathered together all they found, both evil and good, and the wedding hall was filled with dinner guests.

When the king came in and looked over the dinner guests, he saw a man not dressed in wedding clothes, and the king asked the man how he came in without wedding clothes. The man was speechless. The king then told his servants to tie his hands and feet and throw the man into the outer darkness, "in that place there shall be weeping and gnashing of teeth. For many are called, but few are chosen" (Matt. 22:13–14, NASB).

The stone which the builders rejected has become the chief corner stone. This is the LORD's doing; it is marvelous in our eyes. This is the day which the LORD has made; let us rejoice and be glad in it (Ps. 118:22–24, NASB).

The Pharisees sent some of their sharpest students to go with the Herodians to catch Jesus with the dilemma about paying tribute to Caesar. They offered Jesus two alternatives: (1) being disfavored with the people or (2) being disloyal to the Roman government.

The Sadducees were a religious party of Jews distinctive in many of their positions regarding the law, ritual, and doctrine. Examples: (1) They accepted only the written Law as binding and rejected the entire traditional interpretation and development of the Law during the centuries by the scribes. (2) They rejected questions of ritual and did not regard as binding Pharisaic decrees with respect to clean and unclean; in short they rejected Pharisaic tradition. (3) They refused to believe in a resurrection of the body, any penalty in a future life, or any personal continuity of the individual after death.

Paying Tribute to Caesar (Mark 12:13–17; Matt. 22:15–22; Luke 20:20–26)

The Pharisees and the Herodians tried to ensnare Jesus about paying tribute to Caesar. The Pharisees talked together about how they might trap Jesus in what He said. So they sent their best students and the Herodians to say to Jesus that they knew He was truthful and taught God's way in truth, and deferred to no one, being fair to all.

Next they asked Jesus whether it was lawful to pay a poll tax to Caesar. Jesus knew what they were trying to do and responded to them by calling them hypocrites and asking them why they were testing Him. He asked them to show Him the coin used for the poll tax, so they gave Him a denarius. He asked whose likeness and inscription were on the coin. They answered, "Caesar's."

Then Jesus replied that they should give to Caesar what was Caesar's and to God what was God's. When they heard this, they were astonished by His answer and went away.

Jesus Answers the Sadducees about the Resurrection (Mark 12:18–27; Matt. 22:23–33; Luke 20:27–40)

On this same Tuesday, some Sadducees came to Jesus and questioned Him about the resurrection. They didn't believe in the resurrection and constructed a case designed to show problems with the concept of resurrection. Jesus gave a compelling response.

The crowd was astonished at Jesus' teaching, and a certain scribe said to Jesus in return, calling him "Master," that He had answered well because the Sadducees asked Him no more questions.

The Greatest Commandment
(Matt. 22:34–40; Mark 12:28–34)

Having heard that Jesus had silenced the Sadducees, the Pharisees came together and a Pharisee lawyer asked Him a question to test Him. The lawyer wanted to know which was the greatest commandment in the Law.

Jesus told them that the greatest commandment was to love God with their total being. Then, as usual, He gave them more information than they had asked for and told them that the second commandment was to love their neighbor as themselves. There is no other commandment greater than these, and on these two "hang," or depend, the whole Law and the Prophets. The lawyer responded, calling Jesus "Teacher," that He had answered true. Obeying these two commandments was much more than all burnt offerings and sacrifices. Jesus saw that the man had responded intelligently and told him that he was not far from God's kingdom. After that, no one would dare to ask Jesus any more questions.

His Last Public Teaching, the Scribes and Pharisees Denounced (Mark 12:38–40; Matt. 23:1–39; Luke 20:45–47)

Jesus acknowledged to the crowd and His disciples that the scribes and Pharisees had "seated themselves in the chair of Moses" (Matt. 23:2, NASB); therefore, they should do what they said. But they shouldn't act according to their deeds because they themselves didn't do what they said. They made up heavy loads and laid them on the shoulders of men, but they weren't willing themselves to lift even a finger to move them.

The scribes and Pharisees did all their deeds to be seen by men. They had broadened their

He said to him, "'You shall love the Lord your God with all your heart, with all your soul, and with all your mind.' This is the greatest and most important commandment. The second is like it: 'You shall love your neighbor as yourself'" (Matt. 22:37–39, HCSB; cf. Deut. 6:4–6).

Phylacteries

Phylactery is from the Greek and means "safeguard, amulet," because it was thought to ward off evil spirits and ill fortune. To this day Jews call phylacteries by a Hebrew word meaning "prayer bands." Phylacteries were small boxes containing Scripture texts—Deuteronomy 6:4–9; 11:13–22; Exodus 13:1–10, 11–16—worn for religious purposes.

phylacteries and lengthened the tassels of their garment to be seen by men.

Jesus Agonizes over Jerusalem (Matt. 23:37–39)

Jesus said: "O Jerusalem, Jerusalem, who kills the prophets and stones those who are sent to her!" (Matt. 23:37, NASB). Often He had wanted to gather Jerusalem's children to Himself like a hen gathers her chicks under her wings, but they were unwilling. Jesus told them that from then on they wouldn't see Him until they would say, "Blessed is he who comes in the name of the Lord!" (Matt. 23:39).

The Widow's Mite (Mark 12:41–44; Luke 21:1–4)

Jesus sat down and watched how the crowd threw money into the treasury. Many who were rich were putting in large amounts. Then a poor widow came and put in two small copper coins, which amounted to a cent.

The widow put in two lepta worth about 1/64 of a denarius, which was the silver coin worth a day's wages. Thus she put in about 1/64 of a day's earnings

Jesus called His disciples and told them that the poor widow had contributed more to the treasury than all the others combined. The others gave out of their surplus, but she had given out of her poverty and put in all she owned and all she had to live on.

Olivet Discourse (Mark 13; Matt. 24–25; Luke 21:5–36)

Jesus had left the Temple and was going away from it when His disciples came up to Him and pointed out the Temple buildings. Jesus told them to look at the building because not one stone would be left upon another.

As Jesus sat on the Mount of Olives, Peter, James, John, and Andrew came to Him privately and asked Him to tell them what all this meant and what would be the sign of His coming and the end of the age. Jesus told His disciples not to let anyone mislead them because many would come in His name saying that they were the Christ and mislead many.

He said that they would hear of wars and rumors of wars but not to be frightened for such must happen and that wouldn't yet be the end. There would be wars, famines, and earth-quakes; but all that was only the mere beginning of birth pains.

Sign of the Destruction of Jerusalem (Mark 13:14–20; Matt. 24:15–22; Luke 21:20–24)

Jesus said that when they saw the "abomination of desolation" spoken of by Daniel (Dan. 9:27; 11:31; 12:11) standing in the holy place, then those who were in Judea should flee to the mountains. And woe to those who were expecting a child and those nursing babies in those days. He told them to pray that their flight wasn't in winter or on the Sabbath because then there would be a great misery such as hasn't occurred since the beginning of the world.

This section covers Tuesday afternoon to Thursday night of Passion Week, A.D. 30 (or 29) in Jerusalem. Jesus now sought to prepare the disciples for the tragedy of His death and for carrying on His work after His Ascension.

Abomination of Desolation

"Abomination of desolation" appears twice in the New Testament: Matthew 24:15 and Mark 13:14 (cf. Luke 21:20). In both cases the writers quote Jesus' prophetic statements concerning a transgression against the Temple at Jerusalem in which a pagan idol or personage is introduced into the sanctuary.

False Christs and the Second Coming (Mark 13:21–27; Matt. 23:23–31; Luke 21:25–28)

If anyone says, "Look, here is the Christ," don't believe him, because false messiahs and false prophets will come and do great signs and wonders to mislead, if possible, even the elect. He had warned them in advance. The Son of Man will come just as the lightning comes from the east and flashes to the west.

Parable of the Fig Tree (Mark 13:28–32; Matt. 24:32–41; Luke 21:29–33)

Jesus told them to learn from the parable of the fig tree. When its branches become tender and it brings forth leaves, summer is near. Thus, when all these things happen, recognize that He is near, at the door. Heaven and earth will pass away, but His words will not. No one, not even the angels in heaven, knows the day or hour of His glorious return. Only the Father knows the time.

Be Alert! (Mark 13:33–37; Matt. 24:42–51; Luke 21:34–36)

The disciples were told to "take heed," to watch and pray, for no one knows when the time will come. They weren't to be found asleep when He came. And what He said to His disciples, He said to all, "Be on the alert!" (Mark 13:37, NASB).

Jesus told three parables (Matthew 25) to underscore the need to be ready at all times for His return.

The Plot to Kill Jesus (Mark 14:1–2; Matt. 26:1–5; Luke 22:1–2)

The chief priests and the elders of the Jews gathered together in the court of the high priest who was named Caiaphas, and they plotted to seize Jesus in secret and to kill Him, but not during the festival or a riot might happen among the people.

The Precious Ointment (Mark 14:3–9; Matt. 26:6–13; John 12:2–8)

On Tuesday evening, Jewish Wednesday, at the feast in the house of Simon the leper, Mary of Bethany anointed Jesus for His burial.

While Jesus was at Simon the leper's home in Bethany having the evening meal, a women with an alabaster vial of costly perfume of pure nard, or spikenard, came and broke it and poured it over His head.

Some present were indignant and wanted to know why the perfume had been wasted because it could have been sold for more than three hundred denarii and the money given to the poor.

Some of the dinner guests scolded Mary. Jesus told them to leave her alone and not to bother her because she had done a good deed to Him. He told them that they would always have the poor with them and they could do good for them whenever they wanted to; but they wouldn't always have Him. Jesus further told them that Mary had anointed His body beforehand for burial and whenever the gospel is preached in the whole world her deed would be remembered.

Judas Bargains to Betray Jesus (Mark 14:10–11; Matt. 26:14–16; Luke 22:3–6)

Judas Iscariot, one of the Twelve, went to the chief priests to betray Jesus to them. The chief priests were glad when this happened and promised to give Judas money. Judas started plotting as to the best time to betray Jesus.

This anointing has nothing in common with the one recorded in Luke 7:36–50, except the fact of a woman anointing Jesus' feet, and the name Simon, which was a common name. The events recorded in Luke happened in Galilee and this event at Bethany near Jerusalem. There are a significant number of differences between the two events—A. T. Robertson, *A Harmony of the Gospels.*

The events of Mark 14:12–16, Matthew 26:17–19, and Luke 22:7–13 take place in Jerusalem on Thursday afternoon during the day of preparation. They tell of the preparation of the Passover meal at the home of a friend, possibly that of John Mark's father and mother. Wednesday had been a day of rest and was apparently spent with the disciples in retirement in Bethany. Thursday was spent wholly with the disciples until the arrest in Gethsemane after midnight.

Preparing for the Passover (Mark 14:12–16; Matt. 26:17–19; Luke 22:7–13)

On the first day of the Feast of Unleavened Bread, when the Passover lamb was being sacrificed, Jesus' disciples asked Him where He wanted them to go and prepare for Him to eat the Passover. He told Peter and John to go into the city and there they would meet a man carrying a pitcher of water. They were to follow him, and where he entered, they were to say to the owner of the house that "the Teacher" wanted to know where his guest room was so that He and His disciples could eat the Passover. They went and found everything as Jesus had told them.

Passover Meal with the Twelve (Mark 14:17; Matt. 26:20; Luke 22:14–16, 21–30)

That evening Jesus and the Twelve came to the house and reclined at the table and ate.

Of all times, a dispute arose among them as to which one was the greatest. Jesus reminded them that the kings of the Gentiles lord it over them; and those who have authority over them are called benefactors, but this was not so with them. The greatest among them should become a servant. Jesus Himself was among them as one who serves.

Jesus Washes His Disciples' Feet (John 13:1–20)

"Truly, truly, I say to you, a slave is not greater than his master; neither is one who is sent greater than the one who sent him. If you know these things, you are blessed if you do them" (John 13:16–17, NASB).

Jesus knew that His hour had come and that He would soon be going out of the world to the Father. During supper Jesus knew that the devil had already put it into the heart of Judas Iscariot, the son of Simon, to betray Him. He also knew that the Father had given all things into His hands and that He had come from God and was going back to God.

He rose from supper and laid aside His garments and took a towel and wrapped Himself with it. Then He poured water into a bowl and began to wash the disciples' feet and to wipe them with the towel He had wrapped around Him.

Jesus Identified Judas as His Betrayer (Mark 14:18–21; Matt. 26:21–25; Luke 22:21–23; John 13:21–30)

As Jesus hosted the Passover meal, He no doubt reminded His disciples of the events that the Passover meal pictured. After doing this, He announced to the group that one of them would betray Him. They were stunned. Each asked if it were he. Jesus said that it was the one who dipped his hand with Him in the dish. But since all of them were doing this, the betrayer remained unidentified.

Judas asked the question, "Rabbi, is it I?" For those listening carefully, this may have been the clue since the others addressed Jesus as "Lord." But the shock was probably so great, they did not pick up the difference in how Judas addressed Jesus.

Judas' early departure did not tip off the other disciples. He was treasurer, and it was a custom at Passover to buy food for the poor. So they likely assumed this was his mission.

Jesus told Judas to go do what he had to do quickly. And so Judas left the upper room.

Jesus Warns the Disciples About the Coming Crisis (John 13:31–38; Mark 14:27–31; Matt. 26:31–35; Luke 22:31–38)

After Judas left, Jesus warned the disciples about what would soon take place. He told them to meet Him in Galilee when He was raised up. Peter protested that even though the rest of the disciples might fall away, he would remain true. He would stay with Jesus to the death. Jesus told Peter that Satan wanted to sift him like wheat, that Peter would deny Jesus three times. He

Jesus used imagery from Zechariah to describe what was about to happen: "Strike the Shepherd that the sheep may be scattered" (Zech.13:7, NASB).

Therefore, I will allot Him a portion with the great, and He will divide the booty with the strong; because He poured out Himself to death, and was numbered with the transgressors; yet He Himself bore the sin of many, and interceded for the transgressors (Isa. 53:12, NASB).

"This cup is the new covenant in my blood; do this, whenever you drink it, in remembrance of me." For whenever you eat this bread and drink this cup, you proclaim the Lord's death until he comes (1 Cor. 11:25–26).

then consoled Peter by telling him that He was praying for him and was looking to him to strengthen the others after He had returned.

Jesus told His disciples to buy swords. If they didn't have money, they needed to sell their outer garment and buy one. The purpose of the swords was not to take the offensive against enemies but to defend Jesus until He had spent the night in Gethsemane and was then ready to be arrested by those who would fulfill prophecy.

The New Covenant (Mark 14:22–25; Matt. 26:26–29; Luke 22:17–20; 1 Cor. 11:23–26)

As Jesus and His disciples were eating the Passover meal, Jesus took bread, broke it, and distributed it to the disciples. He then commanded them to eat, saying, "This is my body which is broken for you."

He then took the cup, gave thanks, and gave it to the disciples to partake of it.

The Farewell Discourse in the Upper Room (John 14)

Jesus had told His disciples since their retreat at Caesarea Philippi that He would be crucified. The disciples didn't want to hear this and for a time had been able to avoid this harsh reality. But now they could evade it no longer.

Their reaction was profound sadness. And in the discourse in the upper room, Jesus sought to comfort them and point them to the hope that lay beyond the events of the next seventy-two hours.

Jesus responded to questions. He then promised that His disciples would do greater works than He did because He was going to the Father. They would not do this on their own. Jesus promised the Father would send the Holy Spirit who would abide with them.

Discourse on the Way to Gethsemane (John 15 and 16)

Jesus closed His discourse in the upper room saying, "Arise, let us go from here" (John 14:31).

With this, Jesus and His disciples left the upper room and walked to the Garden of Gethsemane. As they walked, Jesus continued teaching.

He likened His relationship to His disciples as that of a vine to its branches. In order for the branches to bear fruit, they must abide in the vine.

Jesus' Intercessory Prayer (John 17)

As Jesus approached Gethsemane, He prayed as a high priest. He first prayed that God would glorify Him and that He would glorify God. Next, He prayed for His disciples to whom He had committed the truth that His Father had commissioned Him to communicate. Finally, Jesus prayed for all those throughout history who would become believers. He prayed for their unity with Him and with one another.

Jesus' Agony in Gethsemane (Mark 14:26, 32–42; Matt. 26:30, 36–46; Luke 22:39–46; John 18:1)

Jesus and His disciples probably arrived at Gethsemane after midnight. He left eight of the eleven at the entrance to the garden and took Peter, James, and John with Him to watch and pray with Him.

Three times Jesus prayed that if it could be possible the cup of suffering might be taken from Him. While Jesus prayed for this possibility, He

Jesus called the Holy Spirit another Comforter or Encourager. The Greek word for another means "another of the same kind as Jesus."

"I have told you these things so that in Me you may have peace. In the world you have suffering. But take courage! I have conquered the world" (John 16:33, HCSB).

Gethsemane was "a garden just across the Kidron brook from Jerusalem. Tourists today may visit such a garden in which stands the Church of All Nations. Gnarled olive trees may still be seen there, and one may view the Rock of Agony, reported to be the very rock on which Jesus prayed"—Hobbs, *The Life and Times of Jesus,* 180.

affirmed that if it wasn't possible, He wanted to do the Father's will.

Luke, the physician, said that Jesus was in such agony as He prayed that His sweat became like drops of blood falling to the ground. His three companions were overcome with sleep from fatigue and sorrow.

ARREST, TRIAL, CRUCIFIXION, AND BURIAL

Jesus Is Betrayed (Mark 14:43–52; Matt. 26:47–56; Luke 22:47–53; John 18:2–12)

As Jesus finished praying, He awoke His disciples. Judas and a band of Roman soldiers and Temple police approached. Jesus asked them who they were seeking, and they said, "Jesus of Nazareth." Jesus responded by saying that He was the One. Judas then came forward and kissed Jesus, a way of identifying to the soldiers who He was. Peter offered some resistance. But Jesus rebuked him.

Examination by Annas and Caiaphas (John 18:12–14, 19–24; Mark 14:53, 55–65; Matt. 26:57, 59–68; Luke 22:54, 63–65)

The band of soldiers and officers who arrested Jesus first took Him to Annas, father-in-law to the high priest Caiaphas and former high priest himself. Annas asked Jesus about His and His disciples' teaching. Jesus said that His teaching had been done openly in the synagogues and in the Temple. He invited Annas to question any of those who heard Jesus regarding the content of His teaching. When Jesus said this, one of the officers struck Him.

Jesus was then taken to the house of Caiaphas the high priest. There the chief priests and many from the Sanhedrin brought false witnesses to bring testimony against Jesus. But the witnesses' testimonies did not agree.

One of the charges brought was that Jesus said He would destroy the Temple and rebuild it in three days. Caiaphas asked Jesus if the charge was true. Jesus remained silent.

Anyone who blasphemes the name of the LORD must be put to death (Lev. 24:16).

Caiaphas then asked Jesus directly if He was the Messiah, the Son of the Blessed One. Jesus answered simply that He was and that all would see the Son of Man sitting at God's right hand, coming with the clouds of heaven.

That was all Caiaphas needed. He tore his clothes and asked why there was a further need for witnesses. He said that Jesus' blasphemy was evident to all who heard His statement and blasphemy was punishable by death.

Peter's Denial of Jesus (Mark 14:54, 66–15:1; Matt. 26:58, 69–27:1; Luke 22:54–62, 66–71; John 18:15–18, 25–27)

Two of the disciples followed Jesus to the house of Caiaphas. One was Peter. The other disciple was not identified by name. This other disciple was known by the high priest, and he entered the house during the proceedings. But Peter stayed outside. Evidently the early morning air had a chill in it because Peter stood in the court-yard warming himself.

A servant girl noticed him and asked if he was one of Jesus' disciples. He denied that he was. This happened two more times with Peter's denials becoming more emphatic each time. After the third denial the rooster crowed, and Peter remembered what Jesus had foretold. He made a quick exit from the courtyard and wept bitterly.

As the day dawned, the Sanhedrin took formal action to have Jesus put to death.

Judas' Second Thoughts and Suicide (Matt. 27:3–10; Acts 1:18–19)

Judas now realized that he had committed a great wrong in betraying Jesus. He came to the Temple and confessed his remorse to the chief priests and other religious leaders. They showed Judas no sympathy. He threw the coins on the floor of the Temple, ran out, and committed suicide by hanging himself.

Jesus Before Pontius Pilate (Mark 15:1–5; Matt. 27:2, 11–14; Luke 23:1–12; John 18:28–38)

Jesus was brought from Caiaphas' house to appear before Pontius Pilate, the Roman governor of Judea. Pilate tried to ascertain the charges brought against Jesus. The Jewish leaders assured Pilate that they wouldn't have brought Jesus to him if He weren't a criminal.

The Jewish leaders charged Jesus with subversion of both Israel and Rome. Two of their charges were designed especially to get Pilate's attention. The first was that Jesus opposed paying taxes to Caesar and that Jesus claimed to be king.

After a time, even with these charges, Pilate could see that there was no case here. So he told the Jewish leaders to try Jesus themselves according to their own law. But they wanted nothing less than the death penalty, and only Rome could authorize that.

Pilate summoned Jesus into Herod's palace and questioned Him further. In the course of the conversation, Pilate learned that Jesus was a Galilean and should be under Herod's jurisdiction. So Pilate sent Jesus to Herod who had heard about Jesus and had wanted to see Him.

Herod had Jesus dressed in a robe and sent Him back to Pilate. When Jesus came back, Pilate told the Jewish leaders that neither he nor Herod could find Jesus guilty of a crime that brought with it the death penalty. Pilate

Pontius Pilate

Pontius Pilate was Roman prefect of Judea from A.D. 26 to 36. Pilate's rule consisted of one provocation of Jewish sensibilities after another. Pilate's permanent residence was on the Mediterranean coast at Caesarea Maritima. He came to Jerusalem only on special occasions like Passover when there was potential for armed rebellion against Rome. While in Jerusalem, Pilate stayed in Herod's palace. The Jewish leaders would not come into the palace because to do so would make them ceremonially unclean and unable to participate in Passover.

While Pilate was sitting on the judge's seat, his wife sent him this message: "Don't have anything to do with that innocent man, for I have suffered a great deal today in a dream because of him" (Matt. 27:19).

The site of the Crucifixion is not known with certainty. At least two places have been suggested: the site of the Church of the Holy Sepulchre and Gordon's Calvary. Hebrews 13:12 says, "And so Jesus also suffered outside the city gate to make people holy through his own blood." Whether the Church of the Holy Sepulchre is on a site that is outside the old city or not isn't certain. Gordon's Calvary certainly is—Hobbs, *The Life and Times of Jesus*, 194.

proposed to have Jesus scourged and then release Him (Luke 23:16).

Pilate's Proposal (Mark 15:6–23; Matt. 27:15–34; Luke 23:13–33; John 18:39–19:17)

During Passover the Romans had a custom of releasing one Jewish prisoner of the crowd's choosing. Pilate thought they might choose to release Jesus, but the crowd made clear they wanted him to release a notorious prisoner named Barabbas.

The crowd became a mob. With growing intensity they called for Pilate to crucify Jesus.

Pilate felt the intensity and knew that his first mandate from Caesar was to keep these people under control. His job, his whole future as a Roman ruler, depended on doing that. Pilate, therefore, took a bowl of water and washed his hands, declaring his innocence of the blood of Jesus.

Pilate had Jesus flogged and turned over to the crucifixion detail. Jesus was required to carry His own cross to the place of crucifixion. The suffering He had endured from flogging and having a crown of thorns pressed into His head left him too weak to be able to carry the cross the entire distance. A Jew from North Africa, Simon of Cyrene, was pressed into service and carried the cross the rest of the distance.

The Death of Jesus (Mark 15:24–37; Matt. 27:35–50; Luke 23:33–46; John 19:18–30)

The Gospel writers described the Crucifixion with an economy of words that all the more communicate the profound solemnity of the event. Jesus refused the drug that was offered to those being crucified. He wanted to face these hours in full possession of His faculties.

Jesus uttered seven sayings from the cross:

1. "Father, forgive them; for they do not know what they are doing" (Luke 23:34, NASB).

2. Two criminals were crucified with Jesus, one on either side. One of the criminals spoke abusively to Jesus. He challenged Jesus to prove His messiahship by coming down from the cross and saving the two criminals. The second criminal rebuked the first by saying that they were being punished justly, but it was obvious that Jesus had done nothing wrong. Then turning to Jesus, the repentant thief asked Jesus to remember him when He came into His kingdom. Jesus replied, "Truly I say to you, today you shall be with Me in Paradise" (Luke 23:43, NASB).

The word *paradise* comes from a Persian word meaning "garden." It is used to refer to the place where believers experience rest and joy immediately after death—Thomas D. Lea, *The New Testament: Its Background and Message*, 270.

3. The only disciple that we know was present at the Crucifixion was designated the beloved disciple and is traditionally thought to be John. He was standing with Mary, the mother of Jesus, her sister, and Mary Magdalene. When Jesus saw Mary, His mother, standing with John, He said, "There is your son." Then he said to John, "There is your mother" (John 19:26–27). From that time John took Mary into his home.

4. From noon until three P.M. darkness fell over the land. Jesus cried, "My God, my God, why have you forsaken me?" (Matt. 27:46). This is the first line of Psalm 22. Herschel Hobbs explored the meaning of this cry: "Was it not that Jesus now had drunk the last dregs of the bitter 'cup'? He had become sin. A holy God cannot look with favor upon sin. In that moment the Son of God wrestled with sin in its deepest depths. The Son of Man, now *become sin*, endured the sufferings of hell as all of the vial of God's abiding wrath was poured out upon sin. It was for only a moment,

"In a very real sense Jesus had by God been left in the lurch, which is itself a good translation of this cry"—Hobbs, *The Life and Times of Jesus*, 199.

but it was the infinite God suffering infinitely for the infinite guilt of finite man" (*The Life and Times of Jesus*, 199).

5. Jesus now knew that His mission had been accomplished and so said, "I am thirsty" (John 19:28).

6. Those in the Crucifixion detail took a sponge, soaked it in wine vinegar, and put the sponge to Jesus' lips. When Jesus took the vinegar, He said, "It is finished" John 19:30).

"It is finished" literally means "it is finished, and it stands finished."

Herschel Hobbs said, "The Greek papyri adds greatly to the meaning of this word (*tetelestai*). It belongs to a family of words which was used in the legal and commercial life of Jesus' day. One word of this family was used to express the idea of completing a legal deed by dating and signing it. In a very real sense, before the foundation of the world, God had drawn up a deed of redemption for all men who would receive it, but the deed had never been dated or signed. So just before Jesus died He inserted the date of His death, and He signed it in his indelible blood" (*The Life and Times of Jesus*, 200).

7. Jesus' final words from the cross were, "Father, into thy hands I commend my spirit" (Luke 23:46, KJV). He let His spirit return to God. To the end Jesus was aware. Death was not something that happened to Him. Jesus reigned even in death.

Signs Accompanying Jesus' Death (Mark 15:38–41; Matt. 27:51–56; Luke 23:45, 47–49)

When Jesus died, the veil in the Temple that separated the Holy Place from the Holy of Holies, was torn from top to bottom. The land was in darkness, and the earth shook. Graves were opened, and some saints who had died were raised from death and were seen in Jerusalem.

The Burial of Jesus (Mark 15:42–47; Matt. 27:57–66; Luke 23:50–56; John 19:31–42)

Joseph of Arimathea, a prominent member of the Sanhedrin, approached Pilate to ask for the body of Jesus. Pilate asked the centurion in charge of the crucifixion detail if Jesus was dead. The centurion answered that He was. Pilate was surprised. He then granted Joseph permission to take Jesus' body from the cross.

Joseph, accompanied by Nicodemus, wrapped Jesus' body with spices in strips of linen cloth and took it to a tomb in which no one had ever been laid.

The next day, which was the Sabbath, the religious leaders went to Pilate to remind him that Jesus had said He would rise from death after three days. They asked Pilate to make the tomb secure until the third day in case the disciples came and stole the body and claimed that He had risen. Pilate responded by providing guards. The religious leaders then saw that the tomb was sealed and Roman guards were posted.

Josephus tells of a quaking of the Temple before its destruction, and the Jewish Talmud even says that such a phenomenon happened forty years before its destruction. This would mean A.D. 30, the very year that Jesus died!

RESURRECTION, APPEARANCES, AND ASCENSION OF JESUS

Jesus' Resurrection (Mark 16:1–11; Matt. 28:1–15; Luke 24:1–12; John 20:1–18)

Before dawn on Sunday morning, another earthquake shook Jerusalem. An angel of the Lord descended from heaven and removed the stone from the mouth of the tomb. The angel's appearance greatly frightened the guards.

While it was still dark, Mary Magdalene came to the tomb. She noticed that the stone had been removed from the entrance, so she ran to tell Peter and John what she had observed.

After sunrise, other women came to the tomb for the purpose of anointing Jesus' body. They expressed concern to each other about how they were going to roll the stone away from the tomb. When they arrived, they encountered two angels. Like the guards, they were frightened. The angels sought to calm their fears. They told the women that Jesus had risen, just as He said. Then they invited the women to come into the tomb and see the place where Jesus lay.

The angels charged the women to go tell Jesus' disciples that He had risen and that He would meet them in Galilee. The women hurried away from the tomb filled with both fear and joy.

In the meantime Mary Magdalene found Peter and John. They ran to the tomb and observed how the strips of linen cloth and burial cloth were arranged. The very arrangement of these items prompted John to believe.

After Peter and John had left the tomb for their homes, Mary Magdalene stood outside the tomb weeping. As she bent over and looked into the tomb, she saw two angels at the place where Jesus' body lay. When they saw that she was crying, they asked why. She told them that Jesus' body had been taken.

Rabboni is Aramaic for teacher.

As she said this, she turned and saw Jesus but took Him to be the gardener. She asked Him where Jesus' body had been taken. At this, Jesus simply said, "Mary."

She knew immediately who He was and turned and cried out, "Rabboni!"

Jesus told Mary to go to His brothers and tell them that He was going to the Father.

The Road to Emmaus (Mark 16:12–13; Luke 24:13–35; 1 Cor. 15:5)

That afternoon Cleopas and another disciple were walking from Jerusalem to Emmaus. As they walked, Jesus joined them. He asked them what they were talking about.

And He said to them, "O foolish men and slow of heart to believe in all that the prophets have spoken! Was it not necessary for the Christ to suffer these things and to enter into His glory?" And beginning with Moses and with all the prophets, He explained to them the things concerning Himself in all the Scriptures (Luke 24:25–27, NASB).

They expressed surprise that their companion wasn't aware of what had happened to Jesus of Nazareth on Friday. They went on to tell of His death by crucifixion and the puzzling rumors that had begun to circulate that His tomb was empty.

The three travelers approached Emmaus. The two disciples invited Jesus to stop and stay with them. Before they shared a meal, Jesus took the loaf of bread, blessed it, broke it, and gave it to them. At that moment they recognized Jesus, and He disappeared immediately. These disciples then returned to Jerusalem where they reported what they had just experienced and learned that Jesus had also appeared to Peter.

"Unless I see the nail marks in his hands and put my finger where the nails were, and put my hand into his side, I will not believe it" (John 20:25).

Appearances to Others (Mark 16:14; Luke 24:36–43; John 20:19–31)

While the disciples were all together behind locked doors, Jesus Himself appeared to them. They were frightened. Some believed they were seeing a spirit. To help them gain perspective, Jesus asked them if they had something to eat. They gave Him a piece of broiled fish, and He ate it.

Thomas wasn't with them on this occasion. When the disciples told him what they had experienced, he refused to believe it.

The following Sunday, the disciples were together, and Thomas was with them. Jesus appeared in their midst and blessed them. Jesus turned to Thomas and invited him to touch His hands and side. Thomas no longer needed to touch. He cried out, "My Lord and my God!" (v. 28).

By the Sea of Galilee (John 21)

Some three weeks later, Peter and four other disciples went fishing one night in the Sea of Galilee but they caught nothing. The next morning they saw Jesus standing on the shore but didn't realize it was He. Jesus asked them if they had any fish. They answered that they hadn't caught any. Jesus told them to cast their net on the right side of the boat. They did, and the catch was so large they could not bring it into the boat.

Jesus invited them to bring some of the fish so that He could prepare them for breakfast. After they had eaten, Jesus asked Peter three times if he loved Him. Each time Peter affirmed his love for Jesus. Following each affirmation, Jesus commissioned Peter to feed His sheep. Jesus then foretold how Peter would die.

The Great Commission and Ascension (Mark 16:15–18; Matt. 28:16–20; 1 Cor. 15:6–7)

Jesus met His disciples at a mountain in Galilee. There He reminded them that all authority in heaven and on earth was His. On this basis they were to make disciples of all nations, baptizing them in the name of the Father, Son, and Holy Spirit, and teaching them to obey all that Jesus commanded. Both His authority and His abiding presence would empower them as they obeyed His Commission.

After his suffering, he showed himself to these men and gave many convincing proofs that he was alive. He appeared to them over a period of forty days and spoke about the kingdom of God (Acts 1:3).

Promise of the Holy Spirit (Luke 24:44–49; Acts 1:3–8)

Jesus and the disciples returned to Jerusalem one last time together. There they may have met in the upper room where they had shared Passover and where Jesus instituted the Lord's Supper. He told the disciples to wait until they had been clothed with power from on high—until the Holy Spirit came upon them—the gift Jesus promised just prior to His death.

Last Appearance and Ascension (Mark 16:19–20; Luke 24:50–53; Acts 1:9–12)

Once again Jesus and the Eleven left the upper room to walk through the streets of Jerusalem. Apparently they went unnoticed by the people of the city, who long since had put the unpleasantness of forty days behind them. The little group went past the Temple area, leaving the city by the Eastern gate, but this time they went on by the Garden of Gethsemane. They continued on up the Mount of Olives, probably following the route which Jesus had taken into the city on his royal entry.

"They had arrived at a place just across from Bethany. There Jesus lifted His hands, and pronounced a final benediction upon His disciples.

And as they were gazing intently into the sky while He was departing, behold, two men in white clothing stood beside them and they also said, "Men of Galilee, why do you stand looking into the sky? This Jesus, who has been taken up from you into heaven, will come in just the same way as you have watched Him go into heaven" (Acts 1:10–11, NASB).

He who testifies to these things says, "Yes, I am coming quickly." Amen. Come, Lord Jesus (Rev. 22:20, NASB).

Even as He was blessing them, He began to ascend into heaven. With eager and longing eyes they followed Him until a cloud obscured their vision, and they could see Him no longer. But their eyes continued to focus on the spot where they had last seen Him" (Hobbs, *The Life and Times of Jesus*, 216–17).

REFERENCES

Hobbs, Herschel H. *The Life and Times of Jesus.* Grand Rapids: Zondervan, 1966.

Lea, Thomas D. *The New Testament: Its Background and Message.* Nashville: Broadman & Holman, 1996.

Robertson, A. T. *A Harmony of the Gospels.* New York: Harper Collins, 1922.